WITH LOVINGKINDNESS
HAVE I DRAWN THEE

Foundations To Transform Evangelism Into Discipleship

DR. LEE ANN B. MARINO, PH.D., D.MIN., D.D.

WITH LOVINGKINDNESS HAVE I DRAWN THEE

Foundations To Transform Evangelism Into Discipleship

Dr. Lee Ann B. Marino, Ph.D., D. Min., D.D.

Published by:
RIGHTEOUS PEN PUBLICATIONS
(The righteousness of God shall guide my pen)
www.righteouspenpublications.com

Scripture quotations taken from The New American Standard Bible®, Copyright © 1960, 1962, 1963, 1968, 1971, 1972, 1973, 1975, 1977, 1995 by The Lockman Foundation. Used by permission.

Scriptures marked KJV are from the Authorized King James Version of the Holy Bible, Public Domain.

Scriptures marked NIV are from the Holy Bible, New International Version®, NIV® Copyright © 1973, 1978, 1984 by Biblica, Inc™. Used by permission of Zondervan. All rights reserved worldwide.

ISBN: 1940197120
13-Digit: 978-1-940197-12-8

Printed in the United States of America.

The Lord hath appeared
of old unto me, saying,
"Yea, I have loved thee
with an everlasting love;
therefore with lovingkindness
have I drawn thee.
— Jeremiah 31:3 (KJV)

TABLE OF CONTENTS

FORWARD

MINISTER, INTERRUPTED

(This blog entry, written on June 8, 2014 shares how my revelation on evangelism all started.)

Me...silent. That doesn't sound right, does it? The two words don't even sound right in the same sentence. It's like me saying, "Me...crying." The truth is that lately I've done a lot of that, too. Me...down. Also not much like me. As I write this, none of it sounds like me. I look at these words and realize they sound like someone else. What I have experienced the past few days, past few weeks...actually, past few months doesn't seem real at times. My response has been...so unlike me.

Of late, I haven't felt much like myself. Some of you can tell that from my statuses. Even before I posted anything on my status about it, I had people coming and asking me what was wrong, because they knew something was wrong in the Spirit. God always has to let people know what's going on, or He knows I won't say anything. I'm a fortress, a "good little soldier," as we used to say. I go through things, and as a rule, nobody ever knows about them. I'm a big advocate of keeping things among those you can trust and not going through everything as a public display. I hate drama, and I hate drama queens. So, I don't talk. In fact, much of the time, people within my inner circle have to drag what is happening out of me. I'll go through it, and through it, and not say anything. I'll still talk, just not about that. I'll still encounter things, I just won't cry about them. I'll feel things, think of things, but I don't tend to respond to them.

Recent things have left me feeling so unlike myself, my response has showed. I absolutely hate it when I am not feeling like myself, and when I respond to things unlike

1

myself. That tends to mean that something is going on that is somehow changing me.

I've had a "Minister, Interrupted" experience: one of those periods where circumstances come along and God uses them to stop us. I was going along on a certain path, fine, and suddenly God interrupted it. "Minister, Interrupted" means it's time to stop just going along because something along that way is either hurting someone else around us, hurting us - or doing both. God wants to alert us so whatever is going on can stop - and in order to do that, He has to stop everything that may be around us.

These events have made me confront myself. I haven't had to confront myself like this in the way that I am now doing for a very, very long time. The last time I remember having an experience like this was when I was young in ministry and trying to evangelize everyone by arguing with them. I used to tell people they had to become Christian because it was right and they had to leave whatever their own religion was because Christianity was better. I couldn't tell them why it was better, or how it was better, and my life and state of being at the time certainly didn't testify that it was better. I just wanted to be right. So, ten years ago, God put someone in my life who not only did not give into my right fight, knowing him challenged me in my methods, approach, and perspective on how to handle a lot of these matters.

When God first started challenging me on these things many years ago, I didn't like it. I did things the way I'd been taught, and those ways were the way I wanted to do them. It wasn't as deep as thinking they were right or wrong; I just didn't want to change. It didn't matter to me that I was seriously isolating myself and nobody could stand to be around me because I was so disagreeable. As God challenged me to start looking differently at things, I had no choice but to change.

Of recent, first while in Europe and now since I have gotten back, the constant challenge to examine witness, impression, and image has been there, yet again. I believe some of this has to do with the new season I have already written about being in, but I believe there is something in here for me to examine, yet again. A recent situation with a very dear friend made me take a good, long look at our own witness of Christianity and what we are making it out to be for those who do not believe. It's also forced me to take a look at those I have around me and why I have them around - especially if signs are there that the people simply don't measure up.

I keep the bar in my own ministry and my own witness very, very high. I am hard on the people I cover when it comes to their ministerial conduct and I am hard on myself to keep a certain standard when interacting with anybody. As God has changed me, I dislike the stereotypes we often hear about disagreeable and difficult Christians, especially when it is thrown around like we are all that way. I feel like when someone makes that kind of a statement, they are saying I am like that, too. The truth is, that is probably not what someone is saying. People are so used to so many judgmental and difficult Christians, they generalize. These generalizations come about because the way one or two people act often define how someone judges the whole of the group. Is this fair? Of course, it's not. I don't want to feel like I am being judged by what someone else does - but the reality is that I am. It's a lovely idea to hope that people will make distinctions, but it's also not that simple. That singular assessment can make or break friendships, relationships, and change the entire course one may be on - all because the wrong person says, does, or behaves in the wrong way. We need to take this seriously because we can be the one person that makes a difference, or we can be the one person who destroys something when it's not our right to do so. We are so focused on evangelism's results (which we deem repentance and conversion), we forget that evangelism is not all about the results we think we should see - they are also about the kind of witness we give, and becoming people who represent Christ in all we do. We need to re-think our witness, our evangelism, and the way in which we seek to approach others because instead of building up, Christians are too often tearing down on things that are of importance, relevance, and connection in people's lives.

Even though I am not a judgmental person, I haven't paid the kind of attention I need to, to those who are around me and those who are considered a part of what I am doing. I live on the principle that working well with others gets a better result than working on stubborn pride. I am this way because I've lived the other way, and it didn't work for me, either. Now my Minister, Interrupted moment is calling me to find a more balanced approach, yet again, on all these matters before me. If people aren't living up to the standard and witness I claim for myself, I need to stop working with them. I need to stop lowering myself and my work to bring it down to a standard that is beneath the call of God on my life. Me lowering that standard in the hopes that people who aren't where they should be will come up higher is not happening - they are simply pulling me down and hurting others around me. In the process, they are hurting me, too.

I'm glad I'm listening to God...through the hurt, through the tears, through the moments of fear, anxiety, and uncertainty...through the moments of transparency, prayer, and yes, crying on unseen shoulders in the Spirit...I am seeing what God wants me to see, and what He is asking of me to do and what He is requiring of me. Most importantly, I am seeing why.

What is God using in your life to create a "Minister, Interrupted" moment? We often run around thinking everything is the devil because it's uncomfortable or awkward. We don't want to feel bad, process, or go through things. We don't want to make change, especially if it means something has to change in us or we have to walk away from some things or people. We cry out to God, but when He gives us the answer, we want to reject it. Reconciliation with others starts as we reconcile with God...only as we look at what He is doing within us and start responding to it with a yes instead of a "It's the devil, I don't like this!"

I thought long and hard before posting this. I decided to go ahead and do it because none of us will get better if I'm not a little transparent. I sincerely apologize to those who have been hurt because I didn't stand up to the ministerial associations I've had or the negative witnesses I've kept around me who were other so-called "believers," and I hope that in some way, while it can't undo what was done, it can make the steps toward whatever bridge can be rebuilt that much easier to take. I can't fix what someone else did, but I can fix in me what needs to change, so I can be better, because I need to be.

Minister, Interrupted. Time to stop, look, listen...and change.

INTRODUCTION

_____

WHY THIS BOOK NEEDS TO BE WRITTEN

Because God has made us for Himself,
our hearts are restless until they rest in Him.
— Augustine of Hippo[1]

The initial process involved to write this book came out of hurt and betrayal on the part of people who were closest to me. As difficult as this experience was, I am grateful for it. It made me see not just who I needed to be, but what I needed to do in response to it. This book is my process; it is my realization that it is not enough for me to change or be different, but the church, too, must change and be different. When I had days that I didn't know what I was going to think, how I was going to get through, or what I was going to do...this book helped me realize the ways in which not only I could go on, but could powerfully triumph in the face of a situation that drove me so low, I had no idea how I was going to get up again.

I got up again. When I did get up again, I realized how much of things needed to change. I looked at me, I looked around, I looked at the general body of believers. I received the care of those who checked in on me and saw a whole new aspect to the world of evangelism that made me realize we need instruction and training in such, in a deeper way.

I've never considered myself the world's best evangelist. In fact, for a good part of my Christian walk, I have not even consider myself to be "evangelical." There have always been staunch differences between the mainline Pentecostal and Evangelical Movements, and I believe strongly in those differences. Whereas the Evangelical community falters, Pentecostalism has always had a stronger base for the answers. It is the reason that, despite many of my own encounters (some of which I will share), I have remained true to the truth present in my faith. This is not to say that I have never had misgivings or questions – but once I experienced the Holy Ghost in my own life, I was never able to change or turn my back on it again.

For the majority of my converted life (since 1999), I have been a strong Pentecostal. While I have made the joke that I have been every variety of Pentecostalism possible: I've been Trinitarian, Oneness, baptized every way possible, independent, Charismatic, Apostolic, and everything in between, I have always firmly believed in the experience of the Holy Ghost as applicable for my life and the lives of others. It is this foundation that has guided my ministry for nearly seventeen years. I have not, however, always been a Pentecostal. For the first seventeen years of my life, I was a Roman Catholic. In connection with this book, the last few years I spent as a Roman Catholic are, in many ways, most relevant.

Telling (at least part) of my story

I was the youngest of five children, all girls, born to my parents in upstate, New York in December 1981. My childhood was, in some ways, very classic of its age. Things were rapidly changing. Technology was expanding, the way we were taught was constantly changing, music was changing, clothing was changing, things were speeding up, and family dynamics were changing. Even the way people worshipped God was changing, as the segue began into what is now classified as the "mega-church" and "televangelist" style of faith and belief. Phil Donahue's popularity began to be replaced by Oprah Winfrey. Nobody had ever heard of reality TV, and movies still had professional actors. Rap, hip hop, and heavy metal began to replace the scene of easy listening music. MTV was not only still cool, it was also innovative, new, and different. The arcade was the place to hang out. Everywhere you looked, change was there: in the streets, on the television, in the schools, in the workplace, in faith and religion, and in the family. There was a sense and spirit of change unleashed on the world.

My parents separated in 1989 and divorced in 1991, thus changing our lives forever. My father was an abusive alcoholic who refused to change and we needed to be away from. This caused me to feel separated from other children my age, even though in hindsight, I was certainly not the only child in my immediate locale with divorced parents. The public nature of my parents' separation and divorce, coupled with a division in the family as a result, made me feel like everyone always knew what was going on in my life. The city where we lived was not that big, and the one Catholic parish we attended was quite small in the scope of the area. Everyone knew everything, and being the daughter of a divorced household was a forever stigma that would not go away easily.

Despite these difficulties, I was intrigued with spirituality. I always remember being interested in God, spiritual things, and religion, even from a very young age. I didn't always understand everything about it, but I knew there was something greater than the things we could see with our natural eyes. By the time I was a teenager, I was strongly interested in religion as a pursuit for life and teaching. I wanted to know God and know about God.

Yes, I wanted to know about God, I just didn't always know where to find Him. From the time I was old enough to have doubts, I always had them about the Catholic Church. Despite years of religious education and Catholic school, my doubts about the church increased, rather than decreased. I learned later on, as an adult, that my mother had them for years – but the doubts we had about the church were not something any of us ever spoke about. The doubts I had were typical among those that leave the church: their negative stance on women's ordination, prayer to Mary and other saints, use of statues, the role of the priest, the pope, and the negatives of church history, which no one could conveniently talk away to me. My doubts about the church would lead me away from the church, then back to it, then away again, then back to it, and then, finally, away for good, all within a period of approximately five years.

Even though I'd been around people of different denominations throughout my life (I went to Presbyterian Sunday School as a young child, Presbyterian Vacation Bible

School as a pre-teen, and, when young, had a variety of friends of different denominations – especially Methodist), I hadn't experienced the sting of evangelicalism much. We were kids, we were young, and religion wasn't something we talked about. In hindsight, I don't ever remember going to school with someone who was not of a mainline denomination – I can't recall any evangelicals among our circles. Growing up in the northeast in the 1980s and 1990s already meant we were relatively quiet on matters of faith, keeping them to ourselves, reserving God and things of faith for Sunday morning services.

My first encounter with the evangelical community came during my second departure from the Catholic Church while in my mid-teens. A nasty encounter with a parish priest sent me – and my entire family – packing from the Catholic Church for a year and a half. It was long enough for me to graduate from the Catholic junior high I attended and start school at a local private Christian school. The experience I had as some semblance of a Catholic (though by no means devout) in this environment was both traumatic and confusing. I went from being in a nearly all-Catholic environment to one where everyone was something else...and being Catholic was treated with disdain and suspicion. I was suddenly being asked if I was "saved" all the time and many questions about what my church believed, which made me very uncomfortable. I'll never forget walking in a classroom one day to find four of the girls in my age group fighting over who was going to take me to church with them first. The final experience came when my history instructor, a former Catholic himself, saw me with a rosary around my neck. His response was, "I have my necklace on today, too," and took out his ski pass.

I left that school after only four months, confused and dismayed, but still unsure of how I felt about my own relationship with the Catholic Church. The doubts I had were re-echoed in this atmosphere, but somehow, the experience made me defensive instead of looking at my doubts. The way these people felt called to "evangelize" made me feel like something was wrong with me that couldn't be fixed unless I did things the way they did them. Differing viewpoints were clearly unwelcome. When it came to why they held the opinions they did, the answer always pertained to the Bible. It didn't matter if the issue was not clearly spoken of in the Bible or even something remotely touched upon in the Bible; the Bible was, according to them, the reason why they held every opinion they had. When having a discussion about any matter, the fact that the Bible was used as a defense for every perspective made it impossible to discuss much of anything, even among themselves. If every conceivable opinion somehow comes down to the Bible, there was no room for an alternate opinion about anything.

They Christians I'd met at this point in time made God seem difficult, argumentative, and ready at any time to "wrestle" with us over issues. Nobody ever told me that God loved me and wanted me to walk in His ways or that He was ready to accept me, as He is a loving Father. They were quick to debate and argue over this or that, all the while making God look like the ultimate master of debate. I had neither the tools, nor the background, to discuss or debate matters with these people. No matter what I was to say, I was not going to say the right thing. Because of their approach, I drove myself right back into Catholicism. I felt as if the faith and world of these people was unreachable for me. My recourse was to return to the Catholic Church a few months later. This is exactly what I did, almost a year and a half after my second absence began.

I didn't return to the Catholic Church because I believe it was true or right, but because it was what I knew. I felt as if the people I'd met made me defend my participation in Catholicism and that the best way to defend myself was to return to the church. My return to the Catholic Church did not abolish my doubts, nor did it give me the sense of security and answers I thought I would find. It was obvious that my absence had been noted. Instead of talking about it, we all pretended it hadn't happened. I was determined to make Catholicism work for me, and I threw myself into church involvement. I was going to find devotions of the church that spoke to me, I was going to embrace the rosary, I was going to go to mass at every possible turn, and I was going to make my Confirmation. I tried to push away my doubts, which, instead of going away, started growing louder and more prominent.

Going to a Christian school had left me an outsider among the Catholics I knew, who liked the types of people I found at the Christian school about as much as the people at the Christian school liked Catholics. Little remarks and references were made here and there when issues about the Bible would come up: how I went to a "Christian" school and that's the reason why I had the perspectives I did about the Bible. The truth was I didn't know how I felt about the Bible, and I surely didn't throw around opinions using Bible verses. Their attitude, however, made me feel as unwanted among the Catholic Church as I had among Christian groups.

During my second return to the Catholic Church, I was also involved with a local non-denominational, "Full Gospel" church because of their extensive youth program. The majority of people I met in that church were former Catholics who broke away from Catholicism for a variety of reasons. As a result, they were often extremely suspicious of all things Catholic, and vehemently anti-Catholic. It was obvious I didn't fit in there, either. Even though they were far more subtle in their attempts to turn me toward their belief system, I was an adventure-project for several of the adults, who passed off their interest to the girls in the youth group. I was bombarded with questions that, although not nearly as offensive as those asked by people previously, still had an underlying innuendo. I was uncomfortable and stopped associating with this church for several years.

I didn't ever really study or read the Bible until I was in college, where it was required reading. I came across many verses that challenged the things I saw in the Catholic Church, and continued to re-emphasize my doubts. Even though I didn't understand a lot of what I was reading when I studied it, many passages which seemed to contradict Catholic teaching left me very uncomfortable. I was in an Apostolic (in doctrine) Christian college, the pursuit of which was not supported by my Catholic counterparts. I was interested in religion, philosophy, and theology, all of which I was studying. I was also very into my studies, and into learning about what other people believed.

In hindsight, I was being drawn away from Catholicism, although I didn't see it like that at the time. The constant wars and drama in my local parish between traditionalists and liberals were getting old, especially as both sides tried to draw me into the drama. I was tired of feeling second-class, and tired of having to report inconsistencies and disregarded regulations to the diocese. I found myself more and more disillusioned with the church. I didn't know what I wanted to be at this point, but I knew somewhere inside that I wasn't going to be able to remain Catholic. Still, I had a position teaching religion in the parish and everyone I knew was Catholic, so I didn't want to leave. I might not have been accepted where I was, but the idea of not belonging somewhere new felt foreign and isolating. I felt that I had too much invested in the church to just up and go somewhere else, so I resolved to stay and try to make change.

I was also exploring different religious systems and found myself far more intrigued with them than I wanted to admit. Almost everywhere I went, I met former Catholics. I considered becoming an Orthodox Catholic after meeting a group of them, because what they did seemed far more ancient than what we were doing in the Catholic Church. I also went on to consider becoming Mormon because the original history of the church was so mystical (I learned more about them later on which changed my opinion) and spent a number of years contemplating Judaism. The fact that other denominations seemed filled with former Catholics made me wonder what it was about Catholicism that seemed to drive people away from it. It was also confusing to me that all these former Catholics felt the answer to belief lied in a variety of different systems, rather than all of them gravitating to one specific system. Some went for something more traditional and ritualistic, while others abandoned tradition and ritual all together.

I knew I wanted to serve God, and that I was called by God to serve Him. The more I researched other things, the more I realized it would be impossible for me to serve God the way I felt called to do so as a Roman Catholic. Still, I stayed, as the battle grew within the parish and the fight increasingly pointed toward me. The more I didn't want to pick a side between the trouble-makers, the more they both started pointing – and turning – on me.

The fight came to an end when I was given two choices by the higher-ups. that they were giving me two choices. Due to all the trouble that would not have a favorable resolution, I was either to leave voluntarily, or face formal disciplinary action. Either way, nothing was going to change. At one point, excommunication was mentioned. This would mean I would no longer hold my teaching position and I would also no longer be counted among the members of the church. I would lose any remaining status I had in the community (which was not much, anyway) and I would also lose all of my friends, because the only thing we had in common was Catholicism. I agreed to leave, voluntarily excommunicating myself from the church. For the first time in my entire life, I was truly no longer Catholic.

Approximately a week later, I found myself interviewing a woman at a non-denominational, Charismatic church. This woman was, yet again, a former Catholic, but carried herself in a different way from those I'd known before. She wasn't pushy, nor was she unkind. She simply talked about her faith and the reasons she was, as she called it, "a believer." I didn't feel like I had to do anything to win her approval. It wasn't a constant debate whether or not I was good enough or could argue eloquently enough – it was just about sharing beliefs – sharing something good with someone else.

Meeting this woman changed my life, because I learned from her influence that being a Christian didn't mean one had to be obnoxious and overbearing. When she invited me to attend service, I accepted without reservation. Within two weeks of meeting her, on February 14, 1999, I was born again at that church, receiving Jesus as my Savior. I received the evidence of the indwelling of the Holy Ghost with speaking in tongues not long after. My experience was completely intellectual: I saw the church and experience of the New Testament in my little church. While it took my heart a few years to catch up to my head, I was able to quickly process information and present that information in the form of debate. I knew what I knew what I knew, and nobody was going to talk me out of it.

My story does not end there, obviously. While some would say that is the pinnacle of experience, it was only the beginning of many years in the faith. I've experienced both joys and blessings, but also seen a lot of heartache and battle. I've spent my years in the faith in numerous philosophical and ethical struggles with other believers. I've watched people fight, stop speaking to others, and reject the Lord because of how others have treated them. I've watched the church fall party to mere politics and money games, and seen numerous believers who once appeared strong fall into states of despair and despondency toward God. I've also seen the faith misrepresented time and time again.

This state of disillusionment has taken me through several Pentecostal denominations (including Charismatic, Word of Faith, Full Gospel, Holiness, Oneness, Apostolic, non-denominational, and now, neo-Apostolic) only to find a consistency of both negative witness and difficulties in faith among most believers today. My own training in evangelism which largely came from Apostolic and Oneness churches was to argue doctrinal points with other people, thinking that argumentation would persuade people to believe as I did. When this method proved ineffective, I pursued it all the harder. I believed in God and believed fervently in Pentecostal Christianity (I love the Lord and have received His Spirit, and I cannot turn my back on that), and I was told such conviction would be enough to persuade people to believe. This never happened. What happened instead is I was considered difficult and argumentative, and nobody wanted to speak with me anymore about anything.

In 2003, approximately four years after my initial conversion experience and numerous runs through different variations of the Pentecostal experience, I met someone who simply would not give in to my argumentative approach. Instead of just up and disappearing on me, he could debate matters as good as I could, and as good as he could get them. I also believed he was genuinely concerned for the future of my ministry, since all I seemed to do was argue with people. In hindsight, the reason the two of us ended our relationship and speaking was as much my fault as it was his; I would not let up.

As a result of that division, God started dealing with me about how I handled matters of evangelism. One day as I tried to use my argumentative approach on someone, the Lord spoke to me. He said, "Lee Ann, people aren't saved because they agree with you. They are saved because of their relationship with Me."

I cried for three days. I was so mad! It was everyone's fault, but mine. I first thought God had some nerve talking to me like that. After all, I was doing all this for Him! Then I was mad at everyone who just didn't come around to seeing my viewpoint on matters. Had they just cooperated, God and I wouldn't be debating like this. The longer I carried on, the more God simply exposed me to myself. I was not doing anyone any favors, nor representing anything rightly the way I was behaving.

My methods of handling people changed, and, as a result, it meant I stopped associating with a lot of groups I had formerly associated with. I also knew as my apostolic call developed that, as an apostle, my call was primarily to the church rather than to the unsaved. Having this realization meant I did not fit in, yet again, with a church full of arguing leaders and the pursuit of denominations where everyone in some semblance or another takes on the characteristics of an evangelist.

I haven't taught much on evangelism throughout my years in ministry. Because I never felt myself to be good at it, I didn't think I had what it took to encourage others to pursue it. That all changed with a situation in 2013 involving, ironically enough, the same person who brought me to confront myself in 2003. By this time, he and I were speaking and friends again. That was all until the woman who was supposed to be my leader, my apostle, at the time, saw fit to attack him. Her virulent treatment of him – which caused him to become sour toward all Christians – made me see just where we are losing people in the Christian vs. non-Christian debate. The Bible teaches us that God draws us with love, not with hate (Jeremiah 31:3). While it is true that every individual person has situations by which they must make choices, it is also true that we aren't the ones who have any right to force them to make decisions outside of a time and place. We, as

Christians, are given the responsibility by God to represent our faith in a certain light. In emotionalism, power and control, and deception, we are failing to fulfill our call as witnesses of His glory and grace to this world.

In wake of the situation, I spent several months talking specifically to non-Christians about their experiences with Christians. I have heard the bad, the very bad, and the very ugly as people shared with me the mistreatment, bigotry, and downright hatred they experienced from people called to proclaim God's love. Not only is this a total contradiction, it is a serious problem.

In listening to the stories of non-Christians, I am reminded of my own experiences early on in my journey. I remember what it felt like to be the odd girl out in a room full of people who made faith seem like a doctrinal wrestling match instead of an experience with God. I remember the confusion and disrespect I felt by people who claimed to be people of God. Remembering how I felt, I can easily understand how people must feel today when people claiming to be of Christ suddenly start acting like the devil because it's time to witness.

This book is needed because we need to change our understanding of evangelism. We need to reorient ourselves to understand appropriate and inappropriate interaction, appropriate and inappropriate reactions, and change the underlying purpose in why we evangelize. Instead of evangelizing in the hopes everyone will become like us, we need to evangelize because Jesus Christ has called us to be light, salt, and hope to a dying world. Instead of focusing on numbers and results, it's time to focus on the impact we are having by focusing on our own actions.

Who is this book for?

Anyone who is a Christian can benefit from this book, from people in the pews to leaders who train and implement evangelism programs in the church. This book seeks to provide a powerful tool in training for evangelism and equipping for the task ahead. While I do not provide every answer for every situation a Christian will face, I seek to provide a basic foundation on which one can become a powerful and purposed witness for the Lord.

If you want to share your faith, this is a book that takes the confusion out of it. There is no reason that evangelism should be approached with such confusion, disdain, and argumentation – which today, it is. I seek to make everyone who reads and enacts the principles in this book delve into evangelism as an extension of something deeper within us. Evangelism shouldn't be something that comes from the surface, but the Kingdom of God within us, moving around us, and dwelling among us (Luke 17:21).

Will this book change my faith?

This book is not intended to be a doctrinal discourse or change anyone's beliefs as pertain to doctrine or theology. This book may change the way you perceive yourself in the struggle for evangelism, and it may change the way you view those you are trying to evangelize. In this instance, that is a good thing. People who need to know of the Lord are not looking for a theological debate. What they may need at that moment may be far different from what you may be trained to give them – and it's time to find a way to reach out and meet needs. Evangelism is about more than just telling someone else what Jesus has done for you, will do for you, or you want Him to do for you – it's about reaching out. Here, you are going to learn about right ways to reach out.

What is wrong with the way we evangelize?

We could start with the fact that it's highly ineffective. Worldwide, other denominations – such as Islam – have far higher conversion rates than all Christian denominations combined. There are a variety of answers why people believe this is. If you ask a Christian, they blame it on the fact that the world is against Christianity and people do not want to hear the truth. If you ask someone else, they say it's the worldwide media presence about different religions. I believe that this may be true on some level, but the reality is that the media representation about religion in general tends to be very negative. While there are exceptions to this, the majority of popular media coverage about any religion pertains to religious extremes: fanatics, swindlers, or people who portray the exact opposite of what a religion claims to be about.

Why do we need to change? Why can't the world change?

Most of us born before 1985 remember the song by Michael Jackson called *Man In The Mirror*. In the refrain, he sings, "If you want to make the world a better place, take a look at yourself and make a change." If we want to see the world change, we have to first look at ourselves and change what we need to change. The Word calls us to be transformed into His likeness. This book is the call – and the way – we can do just that.

I desire to see the church have an impact. We will not have that impact if we do not start to change what we are doing. Daily people stand in the valley of decision. They don't make a decision one way or another because they aren't given the proper information to make a decision. The reason they do not have the proper information is because we are not conveying it. Lost in a maze of rhetoric, denominational disputes, and yes, control – people and their decisions are being lost. Souls at stake are being lost. The answer to solve this problem doesn't begin with them – it begins with us. Thus, let us take the journey together to begin having a life of impact on others.

CHAPTER ONE

IF HE WHO WINS SOULS IS WISE...
WHY IS THE CHURCH SO STUPID?

I like your Christ, I do not like your Christians.
Your Christians are so unlike your Christ.
– Mahatma Gandhi[1]

I can already hear many readers of this book: "Are you saying I'm stupid?" as they read the title of this chapter. No, I don't know you personally, so I can't say that. Read it again, carefully – it says "Why is the church so stupid" – not why is an individual stupid. There is no offense intended in the heading of this chapter – simply an invitation for all of us – as in us in the church – to step back and look at things we are doing incorrectly when it comes to evangelism.

Whenever it's time to talk about evangelism, Proverbs 11:30 inevitably comes up. It is often a foundational verse for the style, approach, and very theme as to why and how people evangelize. Its words, *"The fruit of the righteous is a tree of life; and he that winneth souls is wise."* (KJV) are the mantra, so to speak, of many who attempt to brave the world of evangelism. I think we say it so much we've forgotten what it says and what it is trying to tell us in its meaning.

In all things, I believe God calls us to look at ourselves

first before looking at others. When it comes to evangelism, we are quick to point out all the things we think are wrong with the world. If we are being honest and fair, some of the things we say about resistance to evangelism are justified. There are people in the world who are hostile and intolerant to Christianity for no other reason than they are hostile and intolerant to it. There are many people who don't want to hear the truth about their lives and situations, and don't want the help God offers because His help requires change. Yes, all of these things are true – but there are also lots of reasons why people reject the Gospel message that have nothing at all to do with hating Christianity or not wanting to change. There are all-too-many people who get lost in the spiritual shuffle because a Christian approached them wrong, with a bad attitude, or with lousy answers.

Proverbs 11:30 calls us to look at ourselves first, before we ever open our mouths to attempt to evangelize for the Gospel. If we understand Proverbs 11:30, it will give us an awesome foundation for evangelization.

The fruit of the righteous

The first part of the verse is not the one we automatically think of when it comes to evangelization. We think the evangelism begins with soul winning, but Proverbs 11:30 indicates it starts somewhere else: it starts with the fruit of the righteous. This means that the crux of evangelization begins with our own relationship with Christ – not getting someone else right, but we ourselves getting it right.

The Bible talks a lot about trees and fruit. In fact, the Bible talks so much about trees and fruit, I think we overlook the imagery present. It also doesn't help that the Bible was written in a time where such imagery would be readily understood, and today, well...there are plenty of us out there who would have to make a long trip out to the country (maybe by bus or train) to see a fruit tree. Not being in touch with agriculture hurts our ability to understand this passage in the way we need to so it will make sense to us.

Fruit is the product of something – in a farmer's work, the product that comes forth from a tree. Fruit equates to harvest.

In terms of agricultural understanding, fruit is the product of the harvester's labor. A fruit farmer would spend months at a time – sometimes years, in fact – working and tending to trees in order to bring forth a fruit harvest. After the years of planting, tending, pruning, watering, and growing, the farmer would receive the desired harvest – they would have their fruit, available for eating and marketing.

That fruit was symbolic of more than just mere profit: it also signified accomplishment. The farmer's years of work were seen in the fruit borne from the tree. Fruit represented productivity, dedication, and the years' worth of investment into a tree or trees to bring forth harvest.

It also signified additional work. Harvest meant the fruit was gathered from the trees and vines, and then the real work began. After everything was gathered, the fruit had to become whatever it was going to produce. Grapes were turned into juice or wine, fruit of all sorts were eaten or used for cooking, olives were turned into olive oil, and so on and so forth. The awesomeness of harvest signified an entirely new dimension to fruit and to its productivity for humankind.

This means that "the fruit of the righteous" is the product of righteousness working in an individual's life. For a righteous person to see fruit, they see the production of consistently righteous behavior – the transformation of the individual from glory to glory and faith to faith – over a period of time. Just like the farmer who plants, prunes, tends, waters, and grows the fruit tree over time, so to do the righteous spend that same time investing in God and gaining valuable spiritual skills and insights to become people that are worthy of the name "Christian." While it is its own product, it turns into something else, something greater, something productive in a larger sense.

Righteous...not self-righteous

In order to understand the fruit of righteousness, we need to understand the difference between righteousness and self-righteousness. Simply put: righteousness is something developed in an individual by God, whereby self-righteousness is something developed in the individual themselves. Self-righteousness judges one's own self as superior and esteemed based on their own personal system of rules and regulations. For example: there are some who believe you cannot go to heaven or God is displeased with you if you if you live in a certain country. Some people believe that you cannot be saved if you do not have your own biological children. Some people believe that you cannot be saved if you wear make-up, cut your hair, listen to secular music, watch television, own a cell phone, or if women wear pants.

None of these rules can be found according to Scripture. They are the regulations of men passed off as the rules of God, arbitrarily distorting passages in the Bible to try and fit someone's personal understanding of what it means to be pleasing to God. When people live by this kind of self-righteous judgment, they are unable to reach out to others. They focus so much on exterior, trivial things that have nothing to do with salvation, they are unable to address deeper issues that need to be discussed with someone to lead them to the Lord. Fixing up someone's personal habits is definitely something that may be needed – but worrying over whether or not someone is wearing pants or has a television set is not going to bring anyone to a saving understanding of salvation.

Self-righteousness is dangerous because it makes one believe their right standing with God comes from something they can produce themselves. This means a self-righteous person already considers themselves better than someone else and has appointed themselves a "savior," of sorts, for that person. It also means the individual cannot examine themselves honestly and, therefore, has a disordered relationship with God. They and they alone have given themselves the ability to show the way because they know all the rules and the total way to get someone right with God. They are harsh, critical, judgmental, and overbearing. As a result, nobody ever has the potential to measure up.

Examining self-righteousness in ourselves

Don't make the mistake of assuming self-righteousness is a

characteristic of only certain denominational groups. The examples I gave above are just that – examples. They are given to help each one of you reading this book examine self-righteous tendencies within yourself. What is the first thing you note about someone else? When evangelizing to someone else, what is the most important thing you want to get across? Are you looking to change things in somebody right away, or are you just trying to get someone to stop doing something you personally dislike?

The righteousness vs. self-righteousness discussion exists because the fruit of self-righteousness does not lead to life. It leads to further condemnation, judgment, and above all – it's a negative witness. If you are contending with internal self-righteousness, start by acknowledging it and work with God to start healing it. The healing for self-righteousness comes through humility. When we each step back and realize we are what we are by the grace of God and we have what we have because of the goodness of God, we are able to recognize the righteousness we have is because of the work of Jesus Christ. Then, and only then, can we begin to bear the fruit of righteousness in our lives.

The tree of life

The product of righteousness in our lives is what the Word calls "the tree of life." Interesting, isn't it, that the fruit of righteousness is...an entire tree of life! Wait, that doesn't make sense...or does it? Within each piece of fruit we find seeds contained deep inside, which equate to the budding and growth of yet another tree. From the fruit of righteousness comes the spread of righteousness – seeds are planted toward righteousness in others as the fruit of righteousness is displayed. Even in the oft ignored first part of this verse, Proverbs 11:30 is already teaching us that actions speak louder than words in evangelism.

The Bible is against many things, but one of the major ones is hypocrisy. If we claim to be about the Word and about God and live contrary to those two things, we need to live by our claims. If we aren't living what we believe, we can evangelize with our mouths all day long – we will have no impact on the lives of others. Being good with evangelism is about planting seeds in people's lives with everything we do. This means that as trees of life, we stand forth as something visible people can see that points to life, bearing fruit in season. We showcase righteousness, proving it is possible to live according to God's requirements. In other words – act, live, and do your best, living up to the expectations God has of you. In that way, as a tree of life, the fruit you bear will drop to seed in due season and plant life within someone else for no other reason than because others know you.

Why is it called "soul winning"?

I've always disliked the term "soul winning." I think it makes evangelism and salvation sound like a big game of cards, with people's souls as the ante. If you play your cards right, someone will get saved, and you'll have "won" a soul. I think I came to this understanding because that is the way evangelism is portrayed by people who claim to be "soul winners." It's more about stakes, pride, and ego for too many individuals than truly about helping someone come to a place where they can know God deeply for themselves.

In pursuit of this, I decided to look up the term "soul winning" and see just what it means. It is composed of two Hebrew terms, the meaning of which are:

- **Wins** – *Laqach* which means "to take, get, fetch, lay hold of, seize, receive, acquire, buy, bring, marry, take a wife, snatch, take away."[2]

- **Souls** – *Nephesh* which means "soul, self, life, creature, person, appetite, mind, living being, desire, emotion, passion."[3]

The two definitions of these words are extremely revealing to us about what the Word is talking about when it speaks of "winning souls" or, as is commonly called, "soul winning." In the first place, it is about far more than just getting someone to listen to hours on end of lecture and rhetoric about why you think Christianity is right. The passage is literally speaking of evangelism as a form of spiritual warfare, in which one is battling for souls. It is spoken of as being a means of life for someone else, offering them a way of rescue and an option of safety as they are snatched away from the enemy. It's also not just about saving their soul – but about snatching their entire life, way of reasoning, emotions, mental perceptions, and receiving away from darkness and into life. The very word *laqach* literally speaks of a marriage – that the individual is taken from something and married or taken in marriage to something else – as they come to a place where they are spiritually united with the Lord, no longer bound to anything that seeks to do them harm.

Perhaps a better way to describe what the Bible is speaking of is "contending for life." Any time you engage in evangelism, you are contending for life – spiritual and natural – on behalf of another person. It is a form of spiritual intercession, as you wrangle between heaven and that individual on that individual's behalf. In evangelism, we give people the opportunity to make a choice and come to a place where they too discover life.

Soul-winning and evangelism

I could also title this section, "What is evangelism?" because I am going to define it here, clearly, in connection with understanding what this passage has to do with evangelism. The word "evangelism" literally means "Sharing the good news of Christ." In evangelism, people tell others about the good news of Jesus' life, death, and resurrection, and how this singular Being has transformed all lives who will believe on Him from eternity past to eternity future. The Kingdom of God is also a part of the proclamation of good news, letting people know God's work translates to a living, Kingdom promise therein. Soul-winning relates to evangelism because one contends for souls through evangelism. When we properly evangelize someone, we put them on the path to proper discipleship for life, thus equipping that individual for life (both spiritual and natural). One who has been evangelized unto discipleship has gone from being contended for to living in eternal life. Thus, one who contends for souls has the duty to evangelize. We cannot win souls talking about what Mohammed, Buddha, Krishna, or any other religious leader has done, because none of these individuals lived, died, and rose again for the salvation of mankind. To win souls means to proclaim Christ, and Him crucified and resurrected. If we do this, we prove we are wise.

Wisdom and evangelism

The last part of Proverbs 11:30 states: *"...and he who wins souls is wise."* The last word of the verse is my favorite: "wise." If we are going to contend for life on the front of evangelism, we need to be wise. Wisdom starts with righteousness, continues as we pursue righteous living, and if we are to be effective in evangelism, we need to apply wisdom in our manner and approach.

Being wise (operating in wisdom) means having the ability to be skillful and understanding when it comes to results. When an individual is wise, they have keen foresight: they are able to understand, see, and recognize what will come out of a given situation from many different perspectives. In summary, someone who is wise can see a situation from both an earthly (practical) and heavenly (spiritual) point of view. Wisdom is something to be prized, cherished, and yes, sought after if one is to exercise evangelization as a Christian believer.

If we closely look at Christian history, we can devise evangelization into two categories: wise and extremely unwise. All throughout we can see different people have had different ideas, approaches, and suggestions as to how to handle evangelization. Some of the different approaches to evangelization included:

- Use of force
- Wars
- Baptizing people against their will
- Attempting to fit Christianity into pagan concepts and understanding

- Distortion
- Political pressures
- Bribery
- Deception

Looking at the history of evangelism makes one scratch their heads in confusion. We know the Word instructs us to not handle the Gospel underhandedly (2 Corinthians 2:17, 4:2)...so what happened? "People" is what happened. Lack of wisdom is what happened. The way I like to put it... "stupid" is what happened. With goals, aspirations, and political ambitions, the Gospel got lost in the veil of power and control. It often became a means by which people sought to accomplish something else. In the name of selfish ambition, the Gospel was used, abused, and maligned with sinister motives.

Before you immediately think this list represents evangelism attitudes for a bygone time, the reality remains that people who have the same motives exist today and continue to use the Gospel with sinister purposes. Whether it's an individual who just doesn't know the right way to handle the Gospel or someone who uses Christianity as a campaign platform to win over Christian voters, the Gospel is still used for all the wrong reasons. This leads to nothing more than a negative witness and the number of questions people always have as to how can someone be a Christian when people misuse the Gospel?

The root of such behavior lies in a lack of wisdom. If someone truly understood the power of the Gospel and the power of God, misusing the Gospel would not ever be an option. Unwise behaviors as pertain to religious representation exist in every denomination worldwide. Mishandling that which is sacred isn't unique to Christianity. Singling out Christianity as the only group with this problem is not fair. Every religious group has people who act unwise and act contrary to the doctrine they proclaim. That having been said, it does not make negative Christian behaviors any more acceptable. It means Christians have to be more conscious of how they behave and handle evangelism the same way they are commanded to handle the Gospel – with wisdom.

The Bible commands us to be wise if we want to contend for souls. That means we get ourselves together in a way that can produce results before we ever open our mouths to share the Word with others. We must think out our techniques, what we say, and how we handle ourselves from start to finish, keeping the end result in mind. Even if we don't get the response we seek, we are still called to walk in wisdom, handling the situations at hand. Wisdom gives us the following necessary skills in evangelism:

- **Knowing when to speak, and when to be silent –** People tend to talk too much in evangelism. A good witness is about listening to someone else's thoughts and issues as much as it is about reaching out with specific directives of the Gospel.

- **Examining ourselves** – When I was first saved, I wanted my sister to get saved. Why did I want this? Because I wanted her to come and apologize to me for all the stuff she did and was doing to me, and I wanted her to repent of it all. Most of all, I wanted her to stop doing it and I thought getting her saved was the way to accomplish this. The result was disastrous, and to the best of my knowledge, my sister is still not saved. Before ever opening our mouths, we need to allow wisdom to answer the question: Why do we want to engage in evangelism with this specific person? Sure, we know we are commanded to evangelize to the world, but why are we interested in evangelizing this individual? There can be all sorts of reasons why we might want someone to repent...spanning from for their good...to wanting it for our own good. Sometimes we want to see people come to us and apologize for the things they did wrong. Sometimes we just want people to live differently or stop making us uncomfortable with their differences. Sometimes we just want someone to do what we want or we think is right. What's your motive? If you are moving to evangelize someone for your own reasons, it is going to, most likely, blow up in your face. Evangelism can't be about you or for you. You can't seek to evangelize someone else so you can win an argument; it just doesn't work like that. Fleshly reasons for evangelism equate to fleshly results. If you have an underlying motive for your evangelization, it is best to leave it to someone who doesn't have the motive impacting their actions.

- **Knowing when to start, and when to stop** – Every person who we feel led to witness to may not come around immediately. We've been taught to expect instant results from evangelism's work. Some people take longer than others. We may plant the seeds in someone, but someone else may have what it takes to bring them to a full place of realization. Sometimes it's good to speak, but it's also good to know if you are supposed to stop.

- **Knowing the way to reach out** – Not everyone needs the same style or form of evangelism. I have known people who became Christians simply because they were around someone who had a powerful influence on them. Some people are converted because they see a quality or character in someone who is a Christian, and they desire to have the Spirit working in their lives to produce the same results. Sometimes we are called to go above and beyond, and sometimes we are called to back off. Whatever we are called to do, it is wisdom that guides us to the right movement and method in order to help someone find the Lord in a powerful way.

- **Measuring the Spirit's presence in your work** – Oftentimes, the only way we can measure progress is by the witness of the Spirit. It may not look like, feel like, or seem like we are making progress in the natural. All we can do is follow the Spirit through practical wisdom. Our actions must be guided by the Spirit.

Where is wisdom in evangelism today?

I titled this chapter with a question: If he who wins souls is wise...Why is the church so stupid? After looking at Proverbs 11:30, we understand why we are called to be wise. So the question remains...why is the church so stupid? Why are we evangelizing wrong and missing the world? The church blames the world, but who is really to blame?

I think the lack of wisdom in evangelism boils down to the fact that the church's priorities have shifted. In years gone by, there was a big focus on evangelizing the unsaved. Whether it was via revivals or social efforts (such as efforts to help the homeless), there was a big push to help others know the Lord. The church used to be about actions that spoke of evangelism as much as witnessing with words. Fast-forward to today, the focus of our churches is radically different than they were in different eras. We now see a totally different shift in priorities. Churches are often bigger than they can financially sustain and leaders are preoccupied with finding ways to stay open. Family themes are strong, and churches spend extensive time trying to formulate children's programs and family events to target couples with young children. There is little emphasis on women's ministry (beyond speaking to married women), men's ministry, marriage preparation, singles ministry, and elderly ministry. Discipleship classes or new member's classes are seldom, if ever, taught. The new means of reaching people is believed to be all about a comfortable atmosphere: wearing jeans to church, having coffee available, and not addressing issues that make people uncomfortable. Politics are also strong. Many churches believe the answers to saving the world and evangelizing lies in the way people vote or the candidates that are in office. Instead of building up the Kingdom of God, millions of dollars that could be used to help launch and fuel revival are spent on candidates and worldly legislations.

Evangelism efforts, therefore, seem to be regarded differently than before. In a high-tech age, people consider T-shirts with Bible verses, Christian movies, and Christian-themed pictures on the internet to be enough for evangelization efforts. When people do evangelize, it tends to be in the form of testimony, whereas someone explains what they feel Jesus has done for them. It may also be in the form of doctrinal debate or argument between Christians of different denominations, where one person argues with another over doctrinal differences. No matter how you spin it, evangelism today is regarded in a different vain than it was in the past.

We also don't study or teach evangelization. Bible schools, seminaries, and Christian colleges used to be devoted to the studies of evangelization, hermeneutics, preaching, and exegesis. Most Christian institutes today revolve around the ideas and teachings of one or two people, and have no substance to them; what is taught becomes a copycat of the instructor's ministry. A good number of ministers I've met over the years have never seen the outside of the pulpit, and haven't the first clue about reaching out to others. With no leadership training on evangelism, ministers are unable to train their congregations in effective and purposed methods for evangelization.

Bringing back smart evangelism

If we want to be smart about evangelism, we need to know what we are doing and how to do it. That doesn't happen without good training. It's a mistake to assume that just because someone is a Christian, they have everything they need to evangelize. Good evangelism is the product of individuals who are well-equipped, both in their lives and in the Word, to present the Gospel in a practical way to others.

In the next chapters of this book, we are going to learn how to do that – and understand the principles of wisdom in evangelism, that we may draw the world with loving-kindness rather than methods that have failed time and time again.

CHAPTER TWO

DOES THEOLOGY BELONG IN
EVANGELISM?

*This much is certain, that we have no theological right to set any sort
of limits to the loving-kindness of God which has appeared in Jesus
Christ. Our theological duty is to see and understand it as being still
greater than we had seen before.*
- Karl Barth[1]

Once again, I've started the chapter with a question that
the reader may find absurd. I think, though, that we
need to think about our answer before we speak it:
Does theology belong in evangelism? This is an important
question because the majority of evangelistic efforts often
relate to theological differences between groups. Today, most
debates boil down to theological differences and differences
in doctrinal approach, thinking people will convert because
they are persuaded by doctrine.

I was a student of this theory of evangelism. I believed if I
argued my doctrine well enough with enough supporting
Bible verses, anyone would be thrilled to become a Christian
in the exact same way I was one.

What is theology?

Theology is the scholarly study of things surrounding human beings and their various attempts to understand deity and divinity. It is a part of the study of religion, focusing primarily on the way people understand their concept of the central spiritual being or beings in existence as opposed to studying the entire form of thought surrounding a religious belief. Rather than being about relationship with God, it is the study of the different ways human beings have sought to discover and reach out to their perceptions of the divine throughout history. The true study of theology is not just about the Bible or the Christian perceptions of God, but about the way every culture throughout the world has perceived the supernatural.

When it comes to defining technicalities, definitions, and different beliefs about the divine, the result is theology. Theology exists so human beings can explain their belief systems in both academic and religious circles, and also, to a certain extent, explain and define beliefs for doctrinal purposes. Theology is a scholarly and academic pursuit, something that is typically pursued by those who are in advanced ministry or in advanced academics. Those who come to establish the rules of a certain theological understanding are often individuals who have spent years studying, gathering, and teaching the material they work to define and expound upon.

Theology is not just dependent upon mere belief or the study of scripture, however one may define such. Theology is also a long look at how different cultures have influenced the spiritual beliefs of a people. Over time, theological understandings have changed, wording has changed, and perceptions change. Some things that were the crux and cornerstone of theology a few hundred years ago are no longer relevant today because the way people view that specific issue has changed.

Now we understand theology to be a major in college or a study of things pertaining to God or the gods, but theology is actually the result of thousands upon thousands of years, experiences, and technicalities that have defined its boundaries. It's also important to realize theology is an emerging understanding, and not one that is static or has ceased to exist. With every new generation and every new set of fresh eyes to behold religion in a modern era we find new revelation in the understanding of a theological system.

The limits of theology

Many people think everything in religion or the spiritual relates to theology (we clarified earlier, it does not) and that having a good theological understanding relates to a good understanding of one's faith. Theology, in and of itself, with its own unique purpose, is wonderful. It is a scholarly system, something for theologians, apologists, and others to study, discuss, and debate. It is an intellectual way that scholars are able to sort out many relevant and challenging questions around the divine.

That having been said, it's important to remember that God is not a theology. No matter how technical, advanced, or one may believe in theological wording, the truth is that theology is humanity's attempt to define the divine. No theological definitions, nor understandings, nor terminologies fell out of the sky as we understand them in the study of God or the gods. They are all limited by the bounds of human understanding, study, culture, religious biases and instructions, and the amount of information available to someone within a certain time frame.

Today we find people very hung up on a few technicalities, all of which relate to theology. No matter what theology one espouses, they are drawing on definitions, descriptions, and terminologies that were coined by human beings. Whether they tie back to Scripture or not is another matter relevant to truth, but not to the facts about theology. Every single theological position was thought up through the ages, evolved through a number of processes, and was sometimes voted in or out because of the understandings of those present. Theology does not save anyone; it is not the crux of knowing theology that brings someone into a deeper relationship with God. Theology is a study – it is a scholarly pursuit – and it is excellent in its purpose. Theology on an evangelism level, however, is an entirely different matter.

Relational theory vs. theology

Many years ago, I interviewed a woman about her acclaimed theological belief. Her response to me was, "It's a mystery. Don't spend your time trying to figure it out." As I was not a member of her denomination, such a reply was thoroughly unconvincing to me, not to mention confusing. I could not understand why she would claim to believe in something that she, herself, could never fathom to understand.

Her response was not uncommon. Most people today do not understand the underlying definitions or concepts of their acclaimed theologies. They say they believe something, but they do not know anything about it. In reality, they may believe a form or variance of it, but the everyday average believer doesn't have the theological knowledge to understand the complex theologies they often claim to believe.

To understand theology, one must study it, in and of itself, and gain an understanding of everything that was going on in order to form that theology. While people today debate theology without knowledge, they are missing a vital and important piece of reality in the pursuit to be right. That is the fact that most people do not relate to God in a theological way, but in a relational way.

I understand the need for theology on a scholarly and, even to a certain extent, a doctrinal level. Somehow religious founders and leaders need to put their beliefs about the divine on paper. The language may fail to cover the essence of it all and it also may be so complicated it is almost impossible to make it practical, but it is something that is needed, nonetheless. This is different from someone's relationship with God. The result of theology is complicated – a lot of technical terms about defining spiritualities. The result of a relationship is discipleship unto salvation.

If we are going to evangelize, and do it right, we need to put theology aside in our discussions and debates. What we need to focus on are the relational aspects of faith, by which we make God real and practical to people in their everyday lives. This is because we do not have a relationship with a theology – we have a relationship with a being.

Relational theory is an approach by which something is

understood by a relationship with it. When it comes to God, most people have an understanding of God based on the way in which they relate to Him, and much of the time, by the way they believe He relates to them. This relational aspect of faith is very Biblical, as the Bible is a relational book. The Bible documents thousands of years' worth of interactions between God and His people, the way they viewed Him, and the way He responded to them.

In order to be effective in evangelism, we need to understand relational theory far more than we need to try and pound people with theology. People need to know Him and the power of His resurrection (Philippians 3:10). Both of these are relational, rather than technically theological.

Presenting God as relational

Most people roll their eyes if you jump in a discussion and try to argue theology, because your average person doesn't tend to give theology a lot of credibility. The average person considers theology to be complex and involved, and "over their heads." Someone you are trying to reach for the Lord is not going to be impressed by technical terms or theological brilliance. If anything, their eyes will glaze over and they will either stop listening or become defensive and argumentative themselves.

For example: the debate between Trinitarian and Oneness believers (a debate that has been going on for a very long time) is a theological one, not a relational one. This debate relates to the theological, technical nature of God, not the way one interacts with Him in a personal, relational way. Bringing something like this up to someone who is at a turning point to make a decision about God is not going to help him or her make that pivotal decision.

God is not sitting up in the sky, grading us on our theological notions. He is working with us at all times to make His presence known. To say God is a mystery, as some theological assertions claim, is a total contradiction of the many ways God has revealed Himself to us. If He wants us to be in relationship with Him, then we must be able to find Him and understand Him to a certain degree.

There are a number of different experiences people claim to have as part of their relationship with God. Some people claim to have had incredible visions of heaven or of other things, to have had encounters with angels, and any other number of incredible experiences. These experiences sell books and make for great drama in a testimony or in a Christian movie lacking a plot. Because of the drama associated with them, people can believe they are missing something in their walk with God if they don't have these experiences on a regular basis. As a rule, most people don't have these encounters with God every single day. They are a part of our relationship with God, but they aren't something that most people can relate to.

There are nine core ways in which God is made relational. These are:

- **Types and shadows** – The system of types and shadows is often taught to be exclusively Old Testament and exclusively about prophecies pertaining to Christ, but the truth is that there are types and shadows of everything New Testament in the Old Testament. Beyond the written Word of God, types and shadows are found everywhere in our everyday lives and are often small, unassuming ways by which God reveals Himself to us. A type and a shadow is one thing in the literal that points us to something else in the natural. While typology has been conquered in many ways by theology, types and shadows are just simple reminders that God is with us, around us, and reaching out to us. It can be something as simple as an encounter with someone who confirms something for us, or some little experience that we have that looks one way in the natural, but we know by spiritual perception that there is more there than just what is going on in the obvious. Types and shadows call us to a state of awareness surrounding God's presence, that we may be aware of how and where He is working in our lives.

- **Personality** – The question, "Who is God to you?" is asked frequently in evangelism. While it may seem hard to define this question theologically, it is often quite easy for people to answer it relationally. Many people come to understand God by His nature, especially through the person of Jesus Christ. Knowing God as a loving Father, having that sense of love from Him, or as the grand Creator of the universe, gives people a sense of security in God and a way they can relate to and understand Him. There are so many different aspects to the personality of God and so visible by Jesus Christ, there is truly a way that everyone can understand God for themselves.

- **Experiences with God** – We talked a little earlier about some of the very big and notable ways people experience God, but there are experiences that we can have with God that often go unnoticed or misunderstood. These are often private experiences by which someone knows the Lord has given them a word via an inward witness, a prophet or a confirmation, or something or someone has crossed their path and they know it is God's doing or something beyond anything in this realm, beyond a shadow of a doubt.

- **Spiritual gifts** – In my book *Experiencing God*, I talk extensively about spiritual gifts and the reasons they are important in the life of a believer. Because God cannot be seen physically with the naked eye, we must perceive Him in a different way. The way in which God is known to us is through the different spiritual gifts available to His people. There is no natural or scientific explanation for how these gifts manifest, except supernaturally, by the Holy Spirit. While every believer may not flow in every single gift, most believers walk in at least one or a few of these gifts in their relationship with the Lord. These spiritual gifts are recorded as being word of wisdom, word of knowledge, faith, healing, miracles, prophecy, discernment of spirits, speaking in tongues, interpreting tongues, service, teaching, encouragement, giving, leadership, and mercy (see 1 Corinthians 12:8-10 and Romans 12:6-8). These spiritual gifts can be explained by testimony and something anyone in the Lord can experience.

- **Revelation from the Word** – It is my belief that truly coming to a deep understanding of the Word is only obtainable through a balance of revelation, study, and scholarship. That having been said, most people do not come to a complete or full understanding of the Word in their lifetimes, simply because their reasons for seeking God through the Word tie back to a relationship with God. The difference is level of revelation: having a private revelation of the Word vs. a public revelation. People can read the Bible and come away with a certain level of understanding that can help them through a problem or can find the Bible speaks to them in a certain way because of what they seek to gain from it. The specific revelation they discover may not have much meaning to anyone else besides them, because it is so deeply personal and direct. A level of public revelation relates to teaching about the Word that is sound, truthful, and relatable beyond an immediate personal circumstance.

- **Worship and praise** – Many people find a true depth and experience of God through worshipping and praising Him. In acknowledging His existence, they find His glory and both purpose and answers to issues in their lives.

- **Prayer** – Prayer is simply a communication with God. I am not of the belief that there is a right or a wrong way to pray, or that we have to have to hold certain theologies for prayer to be effective. I think prayer is prayer, and the Word teaches us that those who call on the Name of the Lord shall be saved (Joel 2:32, Acts

2:21, Romans 10:13). People who are curious about the nature of God and learning more about Him should be encouraged to pray and voice their needs and desires to seek more of God.

- **Miracles** – A miracle is something that lacks scientific, natural, or rational explanation for its occurrence. For example, someone who has been unable to walk from birth and is then able to walk again due to faith and prayer has experienced a miracle. There are all sorts of miracles, both those documented and not documented, that have changed the lives of people and show that God is there for us in our need.

Presenting God as relatable

Most people come to understand God as they can relate to Him, not as a technical theology. This means that in order to know how to present God to someone, we have to find out what is important to them. Someone who is a great artist and has never known the love of a parental figure will, most likely, not easily relate to God as our loving Father immediately. They will, however, relate to God as Creator and of God's creative work within us and through us.

Where theology gives a dry description of technicalities, making God relatable makes Him real and understandable to people in their lives. It proves God knows what people are going through and cares about them in their personage and everyday lives. To do this, it is essential that we do the following:

- **Get to know the person you are talking to and sharing with** – People come before the throne of grace with issues. Whether it's growing up with an image and impression of God that's distorted or just an uncertainty about God – or anything else in between – the person that you are sharing with is an individual. It's not right, nor is it fair, to stereotype, demean, or assume you know what someone else is thinking. It's important to dialogue and discuss with someone, to listen as well as talk, and to see what they believe about God as part of the process.

- **Be interested in people** – Don't just act interested, or pretend to be interested. People will feel manipulated and attribute that manipulation to your belief system. In order to be good with evangelism, it's important that you are about more than just the mechanics of conversion (doctrine, beliefs, and a change of mind). The best evangelists and individuals who evangelize are those who truly have a heart for others and want to see others come to a saving knowledge of Christ. They listen as much as they talk – if not more so – and they spend time learning about people and their religious and cultural relevance. They don't feed them various recycled lines about faith and then get angry when they do not accept them.

- **Have a good understanding of differing religious and theological beliefs** – It can be difficult to find comprehensive religious information today because every source seems incredibly biased in their presentation of other people's beliefs. It is as if a constant contrast is being made between the author's beliefs and those they are presenting, even if such is not obviously overstated. It's important to find information about religious groups that is not so tainted, exaggeration becomes an issue. Different groups have different religious emphasis and theological beliefs. Also keep in mind that, within each group, there are individuals who may have their own take on something or who may classify themselves as something, but do not follow all the guidelines or adhere as diligently as their doctrine demands. There are also many subgroups of groups out there which may have differing perspectives on both minor and major points of doctrine, but still claim to be a part of the larger group. Learning as well as listening are both key.

- **Understand evangelism doesn't happen in a short discussion** – Evangelism is the beginning of discipleship. It's not as simple as spouting off some fancy words and leaving someone to their own devices. When evangelism begins, discipleship should follow. If it is not in your ability to take the person that next step, they should be directed toward someone whose ability it is.

- **Remain contemporary about issues and concerns people have** – Too many Christians want to bury their heads in the sand about contemporary issues. Watching all Christian programming, including Christian news programming, does not give a Christian a comprehensive view of contemporary issues plaguing people's minds. It's important to talk to people about what is troubling them, watch the news, and keep current with regional, national, and world events.

The most important theological points in evangelism

Theology as a technicality does not belong in evangelism. This does not mean that it's not essential to have a right understanding of one's beliefs in God before you attempt to evangelize someone else. The reason for this is simple: belief in God needs to be made understandable and relatable, and in order to do that, you need to first know what you believe. It doesn't mean you should create a theological debate, but there are certain things that need to be present in evangelism.

Since "evangelism" means "bearing Christ," that is the main purpose of evangelism. Evangelism is about bringing Christ to people and making Him real in their lives. While I understand it might be tempting to try and win people over based on social positions or some other commonality, that is not the proper nor correct way to evangelize others. Evangelism is not a social call, it is not a political party, and it has nothing to do with a governmental party or how one votes. It has everything to do with Christ. This means as part of evangelization, a proper understanding of Christ must be a part of it.

You can't evangelize without Jesus Christ. That is the main and most important theological aspect involved in evangelism. You, yourself must have a proper understanding of Jesus as the Word made flesh, dwelt among us, full of grace and truth, the very image of the invisible God (John 1:1, Colossians 1:15-18). It is important you see the life and work of Jesus as well as His saving work on the cross. You cannot evangelize Christ if you do not see Him as Savior and if He is not Lord of your life. If you don't understand Him as He is, then you cannot convey that to others.

Given that you can't evangelize without Christ, He is the focus of what we do in evangelism. It's not about deep complexities, but making Christ real and being able to convey this message in a way that people can understand, identify with, relate to, and accept as their own.

Bringing Jesus back down to earth

The whole concept of the Word being made flesh and dwelling among us (the incarnation) is an amazing thing in and of itself. In short, Jesus came to earth as a practical, tangible human being which people could learn from, relate to, and understand. In evangelization, we are called to re-present Jesus Christ in the same way as He was when He lived on this earth: learning from Him, relating to Him, and understanding Him. In evangelization, this means we should focus on three main things:

- The saving work of Christ on the Cross, and His resurrection
- His teachings while on earth
- What it means to become a part of His Kingdom here on earth

Other teachings come as one is made a disciple, as the

issues arise, and as they come to a deeper knowledge of all things spiritual. Evangelism, in and of itself, is a simple thing. While we need to know what we are doing in it, it's not something that is difficult. We need to be practical, relatable, and able to share both our own experiences and uplift the experiences and revelations of others.

CHAPTER THREE

APOLOGETICS AND EVANGELISM

The basic problem of the Christians in this country in the last eighty years or so, in regard to society and in regard to government, is that they have seen things in bits and pieces instead of totals.
- Francis August Schaeffer[1]

In the last chapter, I tackled the issue of theology in evangelism, and reasons why debating theologically are inappropriate for evangelism. Now we are going to turn to the area of apologetics and evangelism. The relationship between apologetics and evangelism is different from theology and evangelism, but the ways both interact with evangelism do have things in common.

What are apologetics?

Apologetics have, through the ages, been defined as the defense of the faith. They are using one's beliefs to provide argument against the doctrinal opponents and enemies of the church. Such is a philosophical method of understanding and defense. Apologetics play off various forms of false teachings that exist in the world in order to defend the position the church holds on that issue and explain why the counterposition is, in some way, in error. Apologetics also provide counterpoints, contrasting Christian understanding of that with non-Christian believers. These foundational elements to apologetics should also be the foundation to every ministerial training (apostles, prophets, evangelists, pastors, and teachers) within the church.

When it comes to the body of believers, apologetics exist to teach ways to remain strong in faith and not be easily swayed by false or erroneous teachers. Apologetics also provide doctrinal and theological matters in ways that make these issues understandable to the average believer.

Apologetics, as ministry work, is for ministerial scholars who labor over the theological and philosophical questions of history and the modern day. They are not a task taken on by average church members, but by apostles, prophets, and teachers who are appointed for the task of instructing, protecting, and defending the Body against invading and errant forces. This work is accomplished through writing, teaching, leadership training, and presentations to the world on church beliefs.

It's been said by many intellectual non-believers that their biggest gripe with the modern church is its lack of scholarship. In many circles, the way people view apologetics has changed in modern times. Many see no reason for apologetics and downplay the important role scholarship and scholarly analysis defends the questions and issues of faith. In an effort to be relaxed and comfortable, apologetics are no longer taught, nor understood. While it is safe to say apologetics are not necessary for salvation, they are a necessary part of maintaining discipleship and working things out so new disciples can grow and seasoned disciples can be made. Apologetics are not more important, nor are they less important, than any other aspect of church leadership and understanding.

How apologetics differ from evangelism

Apologetics are the work of advanced men and women in the faith who are seasoned scholars in Christian matters. The work of apologetics is a work for those in the church. It benefits, builds up, and helps believers to grow in their faith and defend it, as necessary. While those outside the church working on a certain level may pick up something written by an apologist or follow apologetics, the perspective they will have about what is written will be vastly different than one who is a part of the church, having basic and foundational knowledge of Christian faith and belief.

Evangelism is a work directed toward those who are outside of the faith, in an effort to let them know about the awesome promise available to them as they have faith in Jesus Christ. Even though someone might have grown up in church or grown up in a church culture (knowing about things related to the faith), that doesn't mean they have a proper or correct understanding of these things. Evangelism's purpose is not to defend the faith against attack or build up people who already believe, but to reach those who do not believe.

Even though apologetics are not for evangelism, apologetics do cross the path of evangelism in some instances. In the world in which we live, people come equipped with often complex questions about life, the meaning of life, and ways Christianity can change their lives. This is where apologetics and evangelism meet: evangelists should be equipped with the most basic of apologetics to answer the important questions of faith and life that affect people's lives in a simple way.

Evangelism's call to be basic

Evangelism is not a place for complicated and involved teachings, philosophy, or scholarship. It is simply making Christ real and living to someone who has not yet known Him as they need in order to change their lives and enter Him in as Savior and Lord. Endlessly debating over theological and philosophical matters distracts from the matter – or should I say, Being – at hand, which is Christ. In other words – as much as you can, stick to the basics. Don't be on a pursuant crusade to get someone to think exactly like you do about every issue. At the same time, be duly prepared to answer basic questions that can turn complicated as one grows in the faith.

Answering the questions of the faith

I do not believe it's appropriate to get into a philosophical debate about spiritual matters in evangelism. Being that apologetics are formed upon philosophical structure and method, evangelism must take the truth discovered through apologetics and make it understandable for the average non-Christian to understand when questions arise. This sounds complicated, but it's really not. When engaging in evangelism, Christians need to be prepared to answer questions that relate to one's relationship with God. When asked a direct question of this nature, one engaging in evangelism should have an answer or know how to obtain an answer.

Sometimes people come equipped with relational questions. In a world that provides us instant access to so many different religions, philosophies, thoughts, and approaches to life, it's not surprising that people have heard some of them and have some thoughts about those matters. People want to know both how to relate to God and how relating to God can change their own circumstances. Some of these questions include:

- Why does it matter which god I believe in?
- Why should I believe in God?
- Why does it matter if I worship Jesus or someone else?
- How do I know God cares for me?
- What can Christianity offer me that something else can't?
- Where does God fit into my life?
- How should I pray?

These questions are, ultimately, answered by apologetics – but can be simplified by those evangelizing into succinct, poignant answers that can help someone who is new to matters of faith (or new this time around) to discover greater areas of discipleship.

If an issue arises which is too complicated for evangelism or too involved for you to answer, politely and kindly refer the individual to someone who is able to provide an answer. This is the next step for many in discipleship. Refer the individual to a pastor, local church, or other leader who is equipped and prepared to answer the question or questions an individual may have.

Being prepared to answer these questions in evangelism

In order to answer these questions, we all must be trained for evangelism by apostles, prophets, evangelists, pastors, and teachers. These offices help us to see the different spectrums of faith and different perspectives needed to answer questions in the evangelism field. Evangelism starts with good training, the materials of which are provided by solid apologetic sources that can dissect and simplify matters for evangelism's purposes.

Do not think that going out into the evangelism field armed with nothing more than a testimony is beneficial. Yes, testimonies are awesome and are a part of evangelism, but being able to interact and talk with people unto salvation takes more than an impressive testimony. Take the time to study and learn about dynamics essential for good evangelism and a productive path to discipleship.

Later in this book, you will find a question and answer section designed to help answer basic questions that often come up among new disciples or potential new disciples.

Avoiding the temptation to treat every non-believer as an enemy

One final word of caution when it comes to apologetics and evangelism: because apologetics are about defense of the faith, being too engrossed in apologetics without a foundation for evangelism therein can cause a nominal individual to view every non-believing person as a threatening enemy of the church. This is not God's position on evangelism, nor should it be ours. Treating people as if they are a fundamental enemy is going to gain a fundamental enemy. Evangelism is about love, because Christ's work for that person was about love. We must treat people as individuals, not lumping them with larger groups they may belong to. We must approach people, remembering that God loves them – and so do we.

CHAPTER FOUR

LEADERSHIP'S ESSENTIAL ROLE IN EVANGELISM

*And He gave some as apostles, and some as prophets, and some
as evangelists, and some as pastors and teachers, for the equipping
of the saints for the work of service, to the building up of the body
of Christ; until we all attain to the unity of the faith, and of the knowledge
of the Son of God, to a mature man, to the measure of the stature
which belongs to the fullness of Christ.*
- Ephesians 4:11-13

So far, we've looked at evangelism from the perspective of some tough questions and major areas. We started at what we are doing wrong and then travelled to both the issues of theology and apologetics in evangelism. All of the issues we have dealt with thus far have one major thing in common: they all relate to leadership and the way leaders teach on evangelism in the church. If good leadership does not properly equip the church for evangelization, people will, simply put, not evangelize properly.

It's been often said that leaders should be the front-liners of evangelism. Most inquiries made to ministers relate to their numbers of "successful" evangelizations – in other words, how many people have become a part of their ministry as a result of their evangelization efforts. When asking these questions, there are several things we do not consider, nor do we take into consideration. Misunderstandings as pertain to these considerations create judgment among leaders that is both uncalled for and downright wrong. Leaders should never feel pressured to evangelize in order to increase the membership roster of their churches, or be made to feel as if they are doing something wrong if their focus is on something than constant membership increases.

We recognize that in the Bible, the Apostle Timothy was told to *"...do the work of an evangelist"* (2 Timothy 4:5). This command does not mean every office of the five-fold is a by-proxy evangelist, nor does it mean that everyone in the church is called to the office of an evangelist. This means that, even though Apostle Timothy was not an evangelist, everything that he was commanded to do was to be Christ-centric, focusing on the growth of God's Kingdom by introducing as many people as possible to the Lord through evangelism.

It also means that the work of evangelism was something the Apostle Timothy would have been familiar with. Given there are limited examples of the evangelist in Scripture, this means it must have been something he was taught – he learned and acquired it – from the teaching and work of other leaders in the five-fold ministry.

Each office of the five-fold does work that pertains to the building up of the Kingdom of God. The purpose of evangelism is just that: to bring people into knowledge of Jesus as Lord of God's Kingdom. As people come to this understanding, they are better able to understand the different leadership roles and operations of the five-fold ministry as they each contribute to evangelization. Here we are going to look at the different ways each office of the five-fold contributes to the work of evangelism.

Evangelism and the five-fold

The Bible tells us to *"...proclaim the Kingdom of Heaven is at hand"* (Matthew 10:7). This means the Gospel ministry is about more than one thing. It is, first and foremost, about the work of Christ on the cross and proclaiming that work, that all might come to a knowledge of salvation (1 Corinthians 1:23, 1 Corinthians 2:2). But the Word teaches us that the Gospel is not just talking about the death and resurrection of Jesus Christ – it is also sharing about His life, His teachings, His purpose, and the Kingdom work that He has established through His church (the people who are His Body) (Acts 17:11). Evangelism is the first step toward discipleship – bringing people into a place where the work of God instructs them throughout their lives as students of Christ. The goal of evangelism is not to get people saved – it is to get them to become disciples. When one is a disciple, they are not just having a one-time experience with the Lord – they are having a continual experience with Him as they walk in His ways and develop a greater understanding of all He has for them to become. This means being a disciple is about more than just saying a sinner's prayer, or just getting "saved" to avoid hell. That is a very key and important facet in evangelism: getting "saved" is not the goal therein. If we are people of order, then we recognize evangelism is the first step to helping people live lives worthy of the name "Christian" and being in the presence of Christ.

Each unique office of the five-fold holds a specific purpose in this system. It's not a conveyer belt by which people come on and off an altar call, but one by which people learn, grow, and develop for their entire lives, from the moment they come to realize the Lordship of Jesus Christ. When we look at the five-fold ministry in this way, we can see God's beautiful design for it. The church, in and of itself, is not "seeker friendly," nor "emerging," nor "relaxed and comfortable." There is no reason why the church itself, nor entire churches, have any reason to be "special interest" oriented. The church has room for everyone in it: new believers, those who have walked with God for many years, those who are somewhere in the middle, those who are struggling, those who are discovering a greater sense of God's purpose for them, and those who are at new paths, new peaks, and new places. If we will only embrace the five-fold ministry in the way God has intended for us to do so, we will see the church transform itself into the Kingdom-oriented, Christ-centered environment it has been created to become.

In understanding this process, each office of the five-fold ministry has been created to respond to different areas of need present in the church. A seasoned believer does not have the same needs of a new Christian. Discipleship acknowledges the different needs of everyone in the church, and the five-fold sees to it that those continuing needs are met. Instead of bringing people to the Lord and then leaving them to figure it all out, God's Kingdom governance offers the perfect balance needed to see people saved, healed, delivered, set free...and disciples throughout life. To bring this to pass, we need the full-force five-fold ministry of apostles, prophets, evangelists, pastors, and teachers (Ephesians 4:11-16).

The evangelist

The evangelist is mentioned third on the list of the five-fold, but I am starting with it first for two reasons. The first is because this is a book on evangelism and, therefore, this is an office of relevance to the work of evangelism. The second is because the evangelist is often the first office (or the first claimed office) a non-believer will encounter in their experience with discipleship.

Once upon a time, evangelists were associated with travelling ministries. In the 1700s through the middle part of the 1900s, evangelists were individuals who were known for travelling from town to town and holding mass-meetings and crusades in order to bring people to the Lord. In more modern times, people associate evangelists with individuals who have television programs or who broadcast large assemblies and crusade meetings on television. For this reason, individuals who have religious television programs are often nicknamed "televangelists," even if their programming does not fall in accordance with evangelistic protocol. Today most people associate the term "evangelist" with someone who travels to different churches, preaching in them to congregations and groups of churchgoers.

If we step back and try to look at the office of the evangelist from the viewpoint of the Scriptures, the modern-day connotation of an evangelist is not in accord with what an evangelist does. The word "evangelist" literally means "one who preaches the good news about Christ." The Bible indicates the evangelist works primarily with those who are not disciples. They may work with any level of individuals who are not yet disciples: it may be someone who has never heard of the Lord or have no saving knowledge of Him, it may be someone who has a knowledge of Him to a certain extent, but does not have enough right information to make a right decision, or it may be someone who has moved away from the Lord for a period of time or all together. The ministry of the evangelist is to make Christ real to these individuals, proclaiming Him and the power of His resurrection, that those who are not disciple would be interested to become disciples.

It is also the work of the evangelist to both model evangelism and teach the church about evangelism. With a heart to proclaim Christ, the evangelist is the church's forerunner in reaching the lost. They start the process of discipleship, opening up eyes and ears to hear more of truth in Jesus' Name.

The pastor

The pastor is mentioned fourth (after the evangelist), but I am addressing the pastor's role in evangelization because after encountering an evangelist, a pastor is usually the next line of instruction for discipleship. The role of the pastor is to shepherd the people of God, as the word "pastor" literally means "shepherd." This means a pastor leads, guides, and feeds a "flock" (congregation) of people unto discipleship in a local area.

The pastoral office is probably one of the most identifiable offices in terms of history and tradition, but history and tradition have also caused it to be highly misunderstood. People do not understand the placement of the pastor in the work of the five-fold, and, as a result, do not rightly understand how important this office is in the work of discipleship.

In the context of the church, a pastor leads members of one congregation who are not called to leadership (or do not yet know they are called to leadership). Those who have been evangelized and now have a taste of Christ need to understand what to believe and how to live rightly. It is the pastor's job to see that this need is met in the lives of a variety of believers, from the new ones to those who are more seasoned. These individuals in a local community rely on the work of the pastor, his or her continual care, direction, guidance, counseling, and teaching, so they can continue to grow and maintain what God has placed within them in an everyday life context.

The teacher

The teaching office has all but vanished from relevance in modern times. This creates a serious gap in Christian ministry and the work of the church to teach and educate its people rightly. Some argue the teacher is not needed, because we have the pastor. This is an illogical argument. If the teacher was given separate from the pastor, it must serve its own unique purpose for the Body.

Teachers do one thing, and one thing well: they teach. It is the teaching office that sees to it the people of God receive instruction in the truth in a way they can understand and apply. A teacher may teach children, youths, or adults.

In the early years of the church, teachers were often the first instructors of a new convert in the faith. They typically remained their teacher through the maturity process unto faith, to the point where they did not require specific instruction. Today, teachers can play a vital role in the instruction of new converts through individual teaching, Sunday or Bible school classes, answering questions, creating lesson plans, leading New Believer's Class, and assisting others in the five-fold ministry to convey the most important lessons of faith and life to the believer.

The apostle

The work of the apostle is primarily a leadership role in that apostles are first called to train other leaders. While the apostle shares in the duties to preach and proclaim the Gospel, the apostle does not have the same relationship with the non-believer that the evangelist does. While the apostle may preach to crowds or encounter non-believers, giving them the Gospel unto knowledge of Christ as we saw in Acts, the majority of apostolic work begins and ends in the church, building up the leadership and establishing a strong foundation for the Kingdom. Being a training and leadership office, the apostle is called to ensure the various offices and helps of the church know about the importance of discipleship.

The apostle has a unique call in evangelism: the apostle is to be all things to all people (1 Corinthians 9:19-23). This does not mean the apostle makes everyone happy or everyone always likes the apostle. It does mean that the apostle is called to be the one to cross various cultural, religious, identity, and national barriers to reach the nations with the Gospel. God has given the apostle to the church to help the church come to this understanding of being all things to all people. This means the apostle is involved in inter-cultural and social development and growth of the church, so the church's leaders and people are able to reach out to as many as possible, without diversity becoming an issue.

The prophet

Prophets of God have a unique purpose in the Body, and that is to speak the words of God to the people. Prophets may be sent to the believers, the leaders, or those in governmental authority. They call believers to judgment, repentance, and obedience. The work of the prophet confirms the righteous and convicts the unrighteous. It is a powerful work that edifies the church to be strong and seeing of the ways of God.

When it comes to evangelism, prophets proclaim a strong message of repentance. The prophet has a conviction within their message to alert of sin and bring the need for change to the hearts of those who have not yet converted. While the prophet's message may be perceived as harsh to some, the prophet's voice stirs the world to get right with God – believer and non-believer alike.

The prophet, in and of himself or herself, may not be one that is on the front lines of evangelism. They do not tend to be as outgoing as evangelists, and may not always be comfortable in that kind of situation. The prophet, however, can give a powerful word to someone that might reveal a truth and bring a confirmation, and they may have powerful insight into situations that only God can reveal. Prophets also work to keep the church in line, making sure the church herself is ready and prepared to reach out to those in need. We can't bring people to wholeness in faith if we ourselves are in disarray due to sin and evil. The prophet reminds us of God's will for us and God's will, ultimately, for humanity.

Bishops, elders, and deacons

Bishops, elders, and deacons are not a part of the five-fold ministry, but are appointed works to assist the ministers of the five-fold ministry in the operation of the church. Even though these works are not offices like apostles, prophets, evangelists, pastors, and teachers, appointments do play a role in evangelism and evangelistic education.

The word "bishop" literally means "overseer." A bishop is someone who is appointed to oversee something in a local church or ministry by an apostle. This is an important work of stewardship, and must be done with efficiency and purpose. If a bishop is called to oversee an evangelism ministry or street ministry work, for example, they must know about evangelism and have proper training to evangelize and instruct others.

Elders are assigned to assist pastors in education, teaching, and care of the congregations. The work of elders is mentioned as a service to the people, working in instruction, teaching, healing, and general presence. The elders are a powerful representative of the best of church life, people, and work can be. They present an almost "parental" heir in the church, being there for comfort, service, discipline, and education.

Deacons are a ministry of service, both to the church and to leadership. The deacon represents an awesome witness of evangelism through service to the disenfranchised and volunteer outreaches for the community.

The goal of leadership is Kingdom discipleship

If we understand church leadership to have a purpose beyond lining people up and trying to get them to accept altar calls, we can see that God has given us an incredible balance and purpose in ministry. There is literally something for everyone, all needs are met, and all powers are balanced. When it comes to evangelism, each office plays an important role in the work. Instead of turning every office into some semblance of an evangelist, it's important we develop the offices in keeping with their function in God's Word. Then, and only then, will we come to a complete understanding of God's purpose for church discipleship.

CHAPTER FIVE

EXAMPLES OF EVANGELISM IN THE BIBLE

*We should be more concerned with reaching the lost
than pampering the saved.*
— David McGee[1]

B oth the Old and New Testaments are rich in examples
for Christian evangelization. From the Word, we learn
about everything from right and wrong attitudes to the
basic format and approach we can and should have
when it comes to evangelization. The Word even gives us
insight into about what we do when we've done all that is
possible to do.

The Evangelist Philip: Teaching about evangelism through the work of an evangelist (Acts 8)

The Bible only gives us the name of one evangelist, and that
is the Evangelist Philip. We know little of him, save he had four
daughters who prophesied and the Apostle Paul's missionary
team spent time at his house (Acts 21:8). What we do find of
the Evangelist Philip are two discourses of his work in
evangelism in Acts 8.

Therefore, those who had been scattered went about preaching the word. Philip went down to the city of Samaria and began proclaiming Christ to them. The crowds with one accord were giving attention to what was said by Philip, as they heard and saw the signs which he was performing. For in the case of many who had unclean spirits, they were coming out of them shouting with a loud voice; and many who had been paralyzed and lame were healed. So there was much rejoicing in that city. (Acts 8:4-8)

So, when they had solemnly testified and spoken the word of the Lord, they started back to Jerusalem, and were preaching the gospel to many villages of the Samaritans. But an angel of the Lord spoke to Philip saying, "Get up and go south to the road that descends from Jerusalem to Gaza." (This is a desert road.) So he got up and went; and there was an Ethiopian eunuch, a court official of Candace, queen of the Ethiopians, who was in charge of all her treasure; and he had come to Jerusalem to worship, and he was returning and sitting in his chariot, and was reading the prophet Isaiah. Then the Spirit said to Philip, "Go up and join this chariot." Philip ran up and heard him reading Isaiah the prophet, and said, "Do you understand what you are reading?" And he said, "Well, how could I, unless someone guides me?" And he invited Philip to come up and sit with him. Now the passage of Scripture which he was reading was this: "HE WAS LED AS A SHEEP TO SLAUGHTER; AND AS A LAMB BEFORE ITS SHEARER IS SILENT, SO HE DOES NOT OPEN HIS MOUTH. "IN HUMILIATION HIS JUDGMENT WAS TAKEN AWAY; WHO WILL RELATE HIS GENERATION? FOR HIS LIFE IS REMOVED FROM THE EARTH."

The eunuch answered Philip and said, "Please tell me, of whom does the prophet say this? Of himself or of someone else?" Then Philip opened his mouth, and beginning from this Scripture he preached Jesus to him. As they went along the road they came to some water; and the eunuch said, "Look! Water! What prevents me from being baptized?" [And Philip said, "If you believe with all your heart, you may." And he answered and said, "I believe that Jesus Christ is the Son of God."] And he ordered the chariot to stop; and they both

went down into the water, Philip as well as the eunuch, and
he baptized him. When they came up out of the water, the
Spirit of the Lord snatched Philip away; and the eunuch no
longer saw him, but went on his way rejoicing. But Philip
found himself at Azotus, and as he passed through he kept
preaching the gospel to all the cities until he came to
Caesarea. (Acts 8:25-40)

The work of the Evangelist Philip is vital to our understanding of evangelism because through what we can see here of his ministry, we find the keys to handling the Word well unto the end of salvation.

- **Preaching the Word** – Evangelists are what we would commonly call 'true preachers.' While other members of the five-fold might have a gift of preaching, the evangelist's preaching work sits on the front lines of conversion. The heart of the evangelist's message is to preach Christ, as it says the evangelist did. Most people who work in evangelism won't be pulpit or group preachers, but when working in a non-preaching setting, the theme is the same: make Christ known in an understandable, Word-true and sensible, way.

- **Signs** – Those that believe in Jesus shall have signs follow them: drive out demons, speak in new tongues, hold authority over the enemy (pick up serpents), and not be harmed by poisons (Mark 16:17-18). These signs are not just reserved for evangelists or other ministers in five-fold ministry leadership, but anyone who believes in Jesus can display these signs. Signs prove that faith in Christ is real and God is really with them. As a rule, we must remember that signs cannot appear on demand (to satisfy the challenge of someone who is testing God), nor can they just happen because we want them to. Signs are genuine inasmuch as we follow the Lord and we have faith, such appears when it is needed and in its due time.

- **Willingness to go and evangelize** – We can't be effective in evangelization if we think everyone is going to come to us. Yes, people do cross our paths from time to time, but a lot of evangelization is being in the right place at the right time, willing to make the right impact.

- **Ability to understand and convey understanding of the Word** – The Evangelist Philip worked both with a crowd and one-on-one, in accordance with his ministry call. In the instance of the crowd, he preached the Gospel and worked signs and wonders. In the instance of the eunuch, he simply taught. It's important that in making Christ real to individuals we are able to support what we say and make the way of Christ clear and understandable.

- **Preparation for baptism** – The Evangelist Philip saw no reason to delay baptism. There was no reason to sit around, spending six or eight weeks in a baptism class, because the eunuch understood the relevance of baptism. As evangelism is about Christ and the Kingdom, a central aspect of the discipleship process remains baptism. Baptism signifies our death to sin and resurrection to new life in Jesus, thanks to His saving work on the cross. Once someone is convinced of their need for Jesus, they should be prepared for baptism.

The Evangelist Philip also shows us the importance of being adaptable in our approach. Sometimes we may go somewhere with one agenda in mind, but will find ourselves wherever we are for a totally different reason. Our attitude of service is essential to the heart of evangelism.

The Prophet Hosea and his wife, Gomer: Evangelizing through love (the book of Hosea)

As direct and easy as it was to study the Evangelist Philip, the

Prophet Hosea's story is quite a bit more involved. The Prophet Hosea had an interesting purpose in prophetic history. Here was a guy who was called to do the very thing that prophets were forbidden to do: marry a prostitute and live as a type of the spiritual state of Israel's wickedness against God. In the Prophet Hosea's marriage to Gomer, a prostitute, God sent the nation of Israel a loud and clear message about His love for them, the way He feels about the backslider or one who abandons faith, and how we should handle those who are outside or away from the faith God asks us to have. There are a lot of themes in the book of Hosea, many of which are complicated and unrelated to the basic message of evangelism we are looking at in this book. For the sake of space, we are going to look at the themes of evangelism present in the book of Hosea.

When the LORD first spoke through Hosea, the LORD said to Hosea, "Go, take to yourself a wife of harlotry and have children of harlotry; for the land commits flagrant harlotry, forsaking the LORD." So he went and took Gomer the daughter of Diblaim, and she conceived and bore him a son. And the LORD said to him, "Name him Jezreel; for yet a little while, and I will punish the house of Jehu for the bloodshed of Jezreel, and I will put an end to the kingdom of the house of Israel. On that day I will break the bow of Israel in the valley of Jezreel." Then she conceived again and gave birth to a daughter. And the LORD said to him, "Name her Lo-ruhamah, for I will no longer have compassion on the house of Israel, that I would ever forgive them. But I will have compassion on the house of Judah and deliver them by the LORD their God, and will not deliver them by bow, sword, battle, horses or horsemen." When she had weaned Lo-ruhamah, she conceived and gave birth to a son. And the LORD said, "Name him Lo-ammi, for you are not My people and I am not your God."

Yet the number of the sons of Israel Will be like the sand of the sea, Which cannot be measured or numbered; And in the place Where it is said to them, "You are not My people," It will be said to them, "You are the sons of the living God."

And the sons of Judah and the sons of Israel will be gathered together, And they will appoint for themselves one leader, And they will go up from the land, For great will be the day of Jezreel. (Hosea 2:2-11)

The Prophet Hosea lived in an era in which the nation of Israel, as a whole, was completely devoid of God. Israel was immersed in pagan ideals and gods, in complete and total defiance of what they knew to be true. They had been in this state for some time, which means two things. The first thing it tells us is that there were those living who knew God, and just chose not to do what they were supposed to do. The second thing it tells us is that there were those who had been born into the ways of sin, and didn't know the right way from the wrong. The children born to him via his prostituting wife, Gomer, were part of the latter – born into wrong, not knowing better – and his wife was part of the former – knew what she should do, and wasn't doing it.

This spin on evangelism covers two basic groups of people: those who don't properly know God and those who once had knowledge of God, but have departed from it (the "backslider" as they are commonly called). What is interesting about Hosea is the way in which he was called to handle both: and that is with a consistent attitude of loving-kindness (Hosea 2:19, 3:1). It is true that Hosea was called to proclaim the sins of the people and make them aware of their wrongdoing, but the spirit in which he came was one of gentleness and love. Rather than threaten them with hellfire and damnation, the Prophet Hosea's living type reminded Israel – and his family – that God loved them and it was not God Who had changed toward them

When Israel was a youth I loved him, And out of Egypt I called My son. The more they called them, The more they went from them; They kept sacrificing to the Baals And burning incense to idols. Yet it is I who taught Ephraim to walk, I took them in My arms; But they did not know that I healed them. I led them with cords of a man, with bonds of love, And I became to them as one who lifts the yoke from their jaws; And I bent down and fed them. They will not return to the land of Egypt; But Assyria-he will be their king Because they refused to return to Me. The sword will whirl against their cities, And will demolish their gate bars And consume them because of their counsels. So My people are bent on turning from Me. Though they call them to the One on high, None at all exalts Him.

How can I give you up, O Ephraim? How can I surrender you, O Israel? How can I make you like Admah? How can I treat you like Zeboiim? My heart is turned over within Me, All My compassions are kindled. I will not execute My fierce anger; I will not destroy Ephraim again. For I am God and not man, the Holy One in your midst, And I will not come in wrath. They will walk after the LORD, He will roar like a lion; Indeed He will roar And His sons will come trembling from the west. They will come trembling like birds from Egypt And like doves from the land of Assyria; And I will settle them in their houses, declares the LORD.

Ephraim surrounds Me with lies And the house of Israel with deceit; Judah is also unruly against God, Even against the Holy One who is faithful. (Hosea 11:1-11).

Why is this relevant? In modern times, preachers think the way to get people to come unto salvation is to scare them or punitively punish them, representing a harsh and unrelenting attitude toward the person. I suppose the logic is that if a person is afraid of the path they are on, they will want to change. The reality of this, however, is that many people are indignant to such propaganda. Not only does it dissuade them from conversion, it gives a hardened attitude to the situation. People begin to think that if God hates them for what they are doing, they might as well go on and keep doing it, because there's no point in trying to do better. The result is a loss of hope because they do not believe God can love them.

Thus, the Prophet Hosea gives us the following insights into evangelism:

- **Draw with love** – Love doesn't mean that you take abuse or allow people to have an attitude with you. It does mean that instead of threatening, scaring, or intimidating people, you approach them in a manner that is respectful, inviting, and reflecting of God's desire that they come to know Him. Instead of judging people because you disagree with someone about their life or lifestyle, allow God to convict them of matters while you show them how amazing it is to live in the truth of God.

- **Be different** – The Prophet Hosea was willing to obey God unto marrying a prostitute. Think about that for a minute! There aren't too many people who would be willing to compromise their reputation in order to obey God unto this end. The Prophet Hosea married a woman who was not his choice for himself, society's choice for himself, and he had children who reflected the sacrifice he made (who would never be accepted because of this choice). His reality was a difficult one, a life totally wrought and consumed with the work and message God sought to get across to a stubborn people. In summary, Hosea's efforts were different. His life was something people talked about, mused about, thought about, and wondered about. Where are you when it comes to doing different things? Are you afraid to stand out to reach a soul? Do you just do what someone else told you to do in the same way because you don't want anyone to consider you too outrageous or different? Sometimes God calls us to do unconventional things in order to reach people for Him. Being open to being different is one of the best ways we can reach people for the Gospel, because it shows God we have an open heart for His service.

- **Don't make a pest of yourself** – God explicitly told the Prophet Hosea to let Gomer go to her own devices. God did not tell him to make a royal pest of himself, following her around, nagging her, wheedling her, manipulating her, handing her tracts, and being a general irritation to her. No, God told the Prophet Hosea to love her – to seek her out when she was lost and to represent a calm, stable, rational perspective in her life. Too many Christians approach evangelism like they are on a violent quest to seize and conquer people. Give people some space. Love them. Don't annoy them.

- **Never, ever preach hate** – I recognize, even understand, that this is not the world any of us remember growing up. I understand that we may see things today that challenge our sensibilities and may even contradict what we ourselves believe. That does not give us the right to proclaim a message that endorses hate, violence, intimidation, or threats to any group, for any reason. This is contrary to "good news." No matter how much the Prophet Hosea might have disliked what Gomer did, he was still called to love her – not harass her, kill her, or mistreat her.

The Prophet Hosea gives us an incredible insight of the true work God does in souls: He never gives up on us. Even though a time may come when the individual evangelizing someone has to walk away from a situation, we can trust that God will continue to intervene, be it in types and shadows, in someone's life.

The Prophet Jonah: When you don't agree with God (The book of Jonah)

We now move from God's eternal love present in evangelization to God's attention to a story about how He dealt with the hardened heart and bad attitude of a prophet: the Prophet Jonah. The Prophet Jonah is a much-quoted favorite among children's stories, as children are intrigued with the concept of a man living in the belly of a whale for three days. What we often fail to mention in such a story is the reason why the Prophet Jonah wound up in the belly of that whale, and what happened after he got out.

The word of the LORD came to Jonah the son of Amittai saying, "Arise, go to Nineveh the great city and cry against it, for their wickedness has come up before Me." But Jonah rose up to flee to Tarshish from the presence of the LORD. So he went down to Joppa, found a ship which was going to Tarshish, paid the fare and went down into it to go with them to Tarshish from the presence of the LORD. (Jonah 1:1-3)

The story of the Prophet Jonah begins with a call he did not want to answer: one to go and warn the people of Nineveh of coming judgment and destruction if they did not repent. The Prophet Jonah did not want to do this because he believed the people of Nineveh should be destroyed, as they were enemies of Israel. So, the Prophet Jonah got the bright idea to try and out-do God, blatantly disobeying what God told him to do. Instead of going to Nineveh, the Prophet Jonah decided to go in the opposite direction. God's response was to send a huge storm, get the Prophet Jonah thrown overboard, and have him swallowed by a huge fish so he could sit there and think about his disobedience for a few days. In the end, the Prophet Jonah obeyed God, and Nineveh was given the opportunity to repent – but the Prophet himself was still one mighty unhappy character, because the destruction he desired for Nineveh did not, in the end, come to pass.

Now the word of the LORD came to Jonah the second time, saying, "Arise, go to Nineveh the great city and proclaim to it the proclamation which I am going to tell you." So Jonah arose and went to Nineveh according to the word of the LORD. Now Nineveh was an exceedingly great city, a three days' walk. Then Jonah began to go through the city one day's walk; and he cried out and said, "Yet forty days and Nineveh will be overthrown."
Then the people of Nineveh believed in God; and they called a fast and put on sackcloth from the greatest to the least of them. When the word reached the king of Nineveh, he arose from his throne, laid aside his robe from him, covered himself with sackcloth and sat on the ashes. He issued a proclamation and it said, "In Nineveh by the decree of the king and his nobles: Do not let man, beast, herd, or flock taste a thing. Do not let them eat or drink water. But both man and beast must be covered with sackcloth; and let

men call on God earnestly that each may turn from his wicked way and from the violence which is in his hands. Who knows, God may turn and relent and withdraw His burning anger so that we will not perish."

When God saw their deeds, that they turned from their wicked way, then God relented concerning the calamity which He had declared He would bring upon them. And He did not do it. (Jonah 3:1-10)

The story of the Prophet Jonah reminds us of the human element in evangelism. As a type of an evangelist, the Prophet Jonah was called to do something beyond his own comprehension, understanding, and let's just face it: it wasn't what he wanted to do. This important, albeit short book, shows what happens when God calls us to a task in evangelism that we just don't like or see the point of doing – even after we've obeyed God and done it. I like the Prophet Jonah for this reason: he was a human being, with thoughts and feelings about his call, and we are able to see this transparency through his brutal honesty about his assigned task.

- **When you don't like what God is asking you to do...**
  - I have a very hard time believing people who tell me they love every assignment God has sent them on. Things are going to come up in evangelism that you are not going to like. Whether you don't like someone you are called to work with, or you don't like where you are called to evangelize, or you don't like someone in your leadership, or you don't like a co-evangelizer, or the day of the week is not convenient for you, or...and the list goes on and on and on. Sometimes being a good evangelizer means sacrifice. It means doing something that you don't like or think should be done in order to bring salvation to a soul. We've got two options when it comes down to it: if you know God is calling you to do it, you can either do it, or wind up in the belly of a whale for awhile having to have an attitude adjustment.

- **You can't be in evangelism and be a bigot** – The Prophet Jonah had issues with who God called him to go to because he had a bias against them. Being a good witness to the faith means overcoming biases and bigotries to reach people beyond what may be socially comfortable for you as a person. The Kingdom of God knows no race, sex, color, nationality, age, or other social lines that people like to draw in the name of their own social comforts. Tear down the walls if you want to be effective in evangelism.

- **Check your attitude** – Sometimes we can get so caught up in whatever it is we are doing or think we are gifted to do, we begin to forget that our attitudes are everything when it comes to the work of God. The Prophet Jonah clearly had an anointing, but he had prejudice and defiance to go with it. God dealt with his attitude by throwing him into a storm and right into the digestive system of a large fish. Today we like to hear about anointing, but we don't like to hear that God deals with attitude...and the ways He handles bad attitudes are not especially ways that most people like. Ministry, evangelism, service, all that good stuff – is about a lot more than just your gifts or anointing. It's also about how you serve and the attitude with which you serve. If you want to avoid time out in the bowels of a fish...check yourself before you wreck yourself!

- **Are you afraid to be unpopular?** – Paralleling the call to be different, I wonder if part of the Prophet Jonah's defiance of God's call was because he knew the work God had for him would render him unpopular. The People of Nineveh were a hated group among the Israelites, and if the Prophet Jonah was called to proclaim repentance unto them so they might be saved...I've got a sinking feeling all his buddies were not going to look too kindly on what he was doing. He would face people telling him, "Oh come on, that's not God telling you to do that!" and those who would outright reject him because he was now travelling to save a people they hated. Part of evangelism is overcoming the thoughts and concepts of others and walking in the grace of God, that some might be saved. Be prepared for people to reject you because you are walking in faith, that others might hear and receive the Word of God to them.

The wilderness/desert: Evangelism through tough love (Exodus 12-40)

"Therefore, behold, I will allure her, Bring her into the wilderness And speak kindly to her. "Then I will give her her vineyards from there, And the valley of Achor as a door of hope. And she will sing there as in the days of her youth, As in the day when she came up from the land of Egypt. (Hosea 2:14-15)

One of my favorite Biblical illustrations is that of the desert or, in some modern translations, the wilderness. I'm sure some of you reading this are scratching your heads right now, wondering why in the world I would love the Biblical illustration of desolation, waste, and emptiness? That is actually exactly why I love it: because it symbolizes nothingness. The desert was always a place where, in the middle of nothingness – no distractions, no things, no money, no stock exchange, etc. – people found God in a powerful way. There is something about meeting God in a position of total nothingness that allows God to move, unhindered by our limitations on Him, that generates a certain level of power.

You shall remember all the way which the LORD your God has led you in the wilderness these forty years, that He might humble you, testing you, to know what was in your heart, whether you would keep His commandments or not. He humbled you and let you be hungry, and fed you with manna which you did not know, nor did your fathers know, that He might make you understand that man does not live by bread alone, but man lives by everything that proceeds out of the mouth of the LORD. Your clothing did not wear out on you, nor did your foot swell these forty years. Thus you are to know in your heart that the LORD your God was disciplining you just as a man disciplines his son. Therefore, you shall keep the commandments of the LORD your God, to walk in His ways and to fear Him. (Deuteronomy 8:2-6)

We cannot deny, however, that the desert was often used to test people's faith, bring about a place of repentance, or center one's self with God. Whenever the Israelites began to wander unto the foreign gods, they would find themselves in captivity in a wilderness situation, desolate and lacking all the blessings they had before they stooped to idolatry.

When talking about evangelism, we could compare wilderness experiences to "tough love." In an effort to get people to turn the way they need to, God allows people to experience dry times to see how much they really do need Him. It's not so much that God puts them through things, but He removes His hand of provision over them, in accordance with their choice, to allow them to experience the consequences of where their decisions and actions are taking them.

So how do we reach out in evangelism when someone is in a place like this? Remember, the reason someone finds themselves in this kind of experience is so God can reach them, not so they can just sit pretty and make sandcastles in the desert. They are there to come face-to-face with the Lord God.

Then the LORD said to Moses, "Behold, I will rain bread from heaven for you; and the people shall go out and gather a day's portion every day, that I may test them, whether or not they will walk in My instruction. On the sixth day, when they prepare what they bring in, it will be twice as much as they gather daily." So Moses and Aaron said to all the sons of Israel, "At evening you will know that the LORD has brought you out of the land of Egypt; and in the morning you will see the glory of the LORD, for He hears your grumblings against the LORD; and what are we, that you grumble against us?" (Exodus 16:4-6)

The best thing we can do when someone is in a desert place is love them, be there for them, but step back and allow God to work in them. Our interferences can hamper the work God wants to do in them. Instead of trying to fix It or make it better, the best thing we can do is be a positive witness, listen through a situation, and direct them as much as possible toward the revelation God desires them to receive.

Sodom and Gomorrah: When we do our best, and it still doesn't seem to be enough (Genesis 19:1-29)

I think we, as the church, get Sodom and Gomorrah all wrong. We've made it about political issues rather than looking at the real message for us in the passage. The truth is that Sodom and Gomorrah has a powerful testimony in it of intercession and the difficulty in watching people fall by the wayside when they do not heed evangelical efforts.

Then the men rose up from there, and looked down toward Sodom; and Abraham was walking with them to send them off. The LORD said, "Shall I hide from Abraham what I am about to do, since Abraham will surely become a great and mighty nation, and in him all the nations of the earth will be blessed? For I have chosen him, so that he may command his children and his household after him to keep the way of the LORD by doing righteousness and justice, so that the LORD may bring upon Abraham what He has spoken about him." And the LORD said, "The outcry of Sodom and Gomorrah is indeed great, and their sin is exceedingly grave. I will go down now, and see if they have done entirely according to its outcry, which has come to Me; and if not, I will know."

Then the men turned away from there and went toward Sodom, while Abraham was still standing before the LORD. Abraham came near and said, "Will You indeed sweep away the righteous with the wicked? Suppose there are fifty righteous within the city; will You indeed sweep it away and not spare the place for the sake of the fifty righteous who are in it? Far be it from You to do such a thing, to slay the righteous with the wicked, so that the righteous and the wicked are treated alike. Far be it from You! Shall not the Judge of all the earth deal justly?" So the LORD said, "If I find in Sodom fifty righteous within the city, then I will spare the whole place on their account." And Abraham replied, "Now behold, I have ventured to speak to the Lord, although I am but dust and ashes. Suppose the fifty righteous are lacking five, will You destroy the whole city because of five?" And He said, "I will not destroy it if I find forty-five there." He spoke to Him yet again and said, "Suppose forty are found there?" And He said, "I will not do it on account of the forty." Then he said, "Oh may the Lord not be angry, and I shall speak; suppose thirty are found there?" And He said, "I will not do it if I find thirty there." And he said, "Now behold, I have ventured to speak to the Lord; suppose twenty are found there?" And He said, "I will not destroy it on account of the twenty." Then he said, "Oh may the Lord not be angry, and I shall speak only this once; suppose ten are found there?" And He said, "I will not destroy it on account of the ten." As soon as He had finished speaking to Abraham the LORD departed, and Abraham returned to his place. (Genesis 18:16-33)

When morning dawned, the angels urged Lot, saying, "Up, take your wife and your two daughters who are here, or you will be swept away in the punishment of the city." But he hesitated. So the men seized his hand and the hand of his wife and the hands of his two daughters, for the compassion of the LORD was upon him; and they brought him out, and put him outside the city. When they had brought them outside, one said, "Escape for your life! Do not look behind you, and do not stay anywhere in the valley; escape to the mountains, or you will be swept away." But Lot said to them, "Oh no, my lords! Now behold, your servant has found favor in your sight, and you have magnified your lovingkindness, which you have shown me by saving my life; but I cannot escape to the mountains, for the disaster will overtake me and I will die; now behold, this town is near enough to flee to, and it is small. Please, let me escape there (is it not small?) that my life may be saved." He said to him, "Behold, I grant you this request also, not to overthrow the town of which you have spoken. Hurry, escape there, for I cannot do anything until you arrive there." Therefore the name of the town was called Zoar.

The sun had risen over the earth when Lot came to Zoar. Then the LORD rained on Sodom and Gomorrah brimstone and fire from the LORD out of heaven, and He overthrew those cities, and all the valley, and all the inhabitants of the cities, and what grew on the ground. But his wife, from behind him, looked back, and she became a pillar of salt.

Now Abraham arose early in the morning and went to the place where he had stood before the LORD; and he looked down toward Sodom and Gomorrah, and toward all the land of the valley, and he saw, and behold, the smoke of the land ascended like the smoke of a furnace.

Thus it came about, when God destroyed the cities of the valley, that God remembered Abraham, and sent Lot out of the midst of the overthrow, when He overthrew the cities in which Lot lived. (Genesis 19:15-29)

The story of Sodom and Gomorrah begins with Abram, a man who we know was called by God. It was he who, on behalf of his nephew Lot and Lot's family, became an intercessor for these cities, hoping to find any righteous found therein. Abram's actions tell us a lot about not just the work of intercession, but about the work of intercession in evangelism. Whenever someone receives the Gospel, it is in part due to the faithful intercessors who wrangle between heaven and earth for revelation, teaching, and salvation for others.

Since this is not a book about intercession, I want us to look at the role prayer plays in evangelism, and the experience we have when evangelism seems to go awry. At some point in time, everyone who ventures into the world of evangelism experiences someone – or sometimes several someones – who are just not receptive to the Gospel message. It is easy to feel discouraged or like a failure in the face of such a situation, and desire to retreat away from Gospel evangelism.

Abram proves to us that there are many facets to the

spiritual realm that we don't understand. I believe he was firmly appointed to be an intercessor to the people of Sodom and Gomorrah, despite their wickedness, and despite their end. This is something that I can't explain in a way that will make sense to us. I think the bottom line of what we are to learn from Abram's work is that even in the face of the most difficult and trying odds, we must try, anyhow. We don't ever know who our evangelism will reach, or how it will affect others. We must be diligent in prayer, intercession, and our attempts to find even that one who might receive the Word and change their lives.

- **Begin with prayer** – Evangelism should always begin with prayer and seeking God about the right way to approach people. Spending that time in prayer before God's throne helps us to gain perspective into the heart of God and allow His heart to become our own. Evangelism is a process by which we first allow ourselves to be transformed so we can offer others a picture of that same experience. Prayer is still a supernatural means of communication with God and I believe prayer changes us, our perspectives, and our hearts. It prepares us for outreach and those to whom we will reach out.

- **Pray for people who you are going to attempt to reach** – Even if you don't know their names, their faces (God knows who they are), or if you will ever see them again after your evangelism session, pray for people's hearts. Pray for their revelation and knowledge, and for the right words to reach them.

- **Make a point to be involved in the community, knowing what is going on and the various issues and strongholds that are present there** – Different cities, states, regions, and nations have their own specific issues that affect people's reaction to evangelism. If you are in a place that has a serious unemployment issue, there are also other issues relating to drug and alcohol abuse, spousal abuse, and poverty. Knowing what affects an area is important in bringing people hope – and also demands our work in evangelism has a practical component to it, as well. Responding to practical needs is an important aspect of evangelism.

- **Pray and go before the throne, even if it seems hopeless** – The people of Sodom and Gomorrah were beyond redemption. Even though the Bible does not identify their specific sins, it does let us know they were "very wicked" (Genesis 18:20). There was no help to be had for them. Despite this fact, Abram still went before the throne on their behalf, bearing the burden to help them avoid destruction. When the people didn't know what was good for them, or what was ahead for them, Abram did – and he made every effort to ensure they did not meet their own fate. We don't know the full impact of Abram's efforts, but we do know that what he did was both courageous and purposed. Even if you are dealing with someone or someone who has a situation that seems hopeless, bring it before the throne and persistently seek God's face until you are able to see an answer.

- **Never underestimate the by-standards** – I wonder if it truly was nothing more than Abram's intercession that got Lot's family out of Sodom and Gomorrah alive. Even though the whole of the area was not saved, Lot's family was. This is regardless of whatever issues they may have had as themselves – Abram's intercession insured Lot's family through the destruction of two cities. Even though you may not see the results you hope for, every soul, every person, every one that you reach (or is reached by proxy) is relevant to God.

- **Why evangelism doesn't work all of the time** – We need to understand that there are many, many reasons why someone may be resistant to evangelical efforts.

Many times we blame ourselves, but I believe the story of Abram is present in the Bible to remind us that people can be resistant to the spirit of conversion for any variety of reasons. This is especially true if the resistance seems to come with no other cause.

- **A spirit of rebellion** – The Bible tells us that the people of Sodom were very wicked. In their state of wickedness, they were not about to turn aside to obedience. Everything one does when in a state of wickedness equates to rebellion, because it is done out of a contrary spirit against God most high. When someone is like this, in outright and open rebellion, they are going to automatically resist evangelical efforts in the Gospel.

- **Misunderstanding** – Whenever we carry the Gospel to someone else, communication is key. Sometimes we don't communicate the way we want, nor the way we intend. If we aren't clear on something, something seems to be misunderstood, it's better to take a deep breath, step back, clarify, or leave the door open to continue the conversation at a later time.

- **Negative prior experiences** – Whether right or wrong, people judge others by the experiences they've had with a group based on their interactions had with another or others of the same group. People who aren't Christian or who perhaps once were but had a certain experience with other Christians often do judge all Christians based upon those experiences. Someone may very well judge you based on how someone else who claimed to be a Christian also treated them. With such people, it's important to emphasize differences between people and empathize with such an experience.

- **Stereotypes** – "All Christians are obnoxious." "All Christians are loud." "All Christians are Republicans."

"All Christians follow the pope." "All Christians hate people who are different from them." These statements are examples of stereotyping against Christians. Stereotypes exist when an individual stigmatizes an entire group of people based on the beliefs of one or a very vocal portion of that group. Christians today are stigmatized based on many stereotypes, some of which are found above. The best way to overcome stereotypes is to present the truth about them by an outward witness against them.

- **They just aren't quite there yet** – Sometimes people have been presented all the information they need to make a decision of faith, but they are not ready to make that final step. I don't know that there is a specific reason why people debate with this, or if it is simply something that some people just wrestle with more than others. Whatever the reason, these individuals are just not ready to take the leap into faith.

- **Called to sow the seeds but not see the harvest at this time** – When we meet someone, odds are good they are at some point along their journey with faith. Some might be at the beginning, others might be at some point in the middle, and others might be right at the end. Sometimes we may not be the one who sees the harvest of conversion. We might start the process, and someone else might be able to provide that final push to bring them to repentance and belief.

Why we looked specifically at examples of Biblical evangelism

There are, obviously, numerous other examples of evangelism in the Bible than we have examined here. The reason I selected these passages on evangelism is because they show us a vast perspective on evangelism and the results which may emerge. Some are dependent on us, some are intricately related to the situations which exist surrounding evangelism, some are dependent upon those who choose to reject the message, and some are related to the place where someone might be in their process of faith. Whatever circumstance you are faced with in evangelism, the Word offers a perspective that can help inspire you and keep you on a right track for witnessing.

CHAPTER SIX

WITNESSING WITHOUT SAYING A WORD

*If you Christians want me to believe in your redeemer,
you're going to have to learn how to look more redeemed.*
- Friedrich W. Nietzsche[1]

Francis of Assisi said, *"Preach the Gospel at all times. If necessary, use words."* Looking at his words and those written by Friedrich Nietzsche above should cause every one of us to stop and pause. In that pause, we need to ask ourselves about the witness of our lives...and just what we are saying with our lives when we aren't consciously trying to evangelize other people.

No smoking. No drinking. No drugs. No sex outside of marriage. No wild parties. No promiscuous clothing. Over the past fifty years, many of the rules people used to associate with Christians began to disintegrate. One of the biggest arguments in favor of moving away from several of these regulations was the belief that people can follow exterior, outward rules without transformation of the heart. Couple this with the fact that some people took rules and regulations to the ultimate extreme and began imposing nothing more than legalism on people, the response to this examination was to abandon all rules and regulations for believers, not adhering to any standards or guidelines for signs of a true believer.

It is true that people can just follow rules without any meaning behind them. I was a member of a church for years and did just that – followed many arbitrary rules – simply because they were imposed upon me. When I started to think about many of them, I tried to find ways to get around them. It's obvious in looking at history that I was not alone in that pursuit. I am the first to admit, even support the belief that following a bunch of rules will not save us. At the same time, I think we need to find a balanced perspective between living and doing whatever we want and blaming that on God and living with many man-made rules and passing those off as of God, as well. We need to step back and realize that the middle ground – that balance – is where we will hear from God and come to a point where our witness is not in jeopardy due to our behavior.

Erosion of our life witness

It's obvious the church is confused about the conduct we are supposed to have as believers. We've switched our focus from our conduct to what rules we should obey and whether or not rules and regulations are relevant. Because Christians are unable to agree about basic points of believer conduct, we've seen a steady decline in behavior we could define as "witness worthy" in recent years. Many have abandoned any sense of Christian conduct all together, while others have gone to the opposite extreme and become more rigid and legalistic than ever. In both extremes, we are losing witness.

We are witnessing to people before we ever open our mouths, before we ever utter a word about Jesus, and long before we ever get bold enough to let someone else know we are a Christian. People are making judgments and assessments about us in our attire, our habits, the way we speak and interact with other people, the things that amuse and entertain us, and the overall way we carry ourselves and treat other people. Yes, it is important what we say in evangelism and how we approach people – but it is far more important that we remember our lives are a witness, whether we are trying to win souls, or not.

Faith vs. works debate

For nearly six hundred years, the church has been in an uproar over the issue of faith and works. What do works do? Do works save us? Are we saved by our works? Are we saved by our faith? Do we need works? Are unsaved people saved by their works? Some churches teach that we will be saved by the good we do. Some churches teach that only faith saves us. Who is right, and who is wrong...or more importantly...when it comes to works, is any of this relevant?

What use is it, my brethren, if someone says he has faith but he has no works? Can that faith save him? If a brother or sister is without clothing and in need of daily food, and one of you says to them, "Go in peace, be warmed and be filled," and yet you do not give them what is necessary for their body, what use is that? Even so faith, if it has no works, is dead, being by itself.

But someone may well say, "You have faith and I have works; show me your faith without the works, and I will show you my faith by my works." You believe that God is one. You do well; the demons also believe, and shudder. But are you willing to recognize, you foolish fellow, that faith without works is useless? Was not Abraham our father justified by works when he offered up Isaac his son on the altar? [22] You see that faith was working with his works, and as a result of the works, faith was perfected; and the Scripture was fulfilled which says, "AND ABRAHAM BELIEVED GOD, AND IT WAS RECKONED TO HIM AS RIGHTEOUSNESS," and he was called the friend of God. You see that a man is justified by works and not by faith alone. In the same way, was not Rahab the harlot also justified by works when she received the messengers and sent them out by another way? For just as the body without the spirit is dead, so also faith without works is dead. (James 2:14-26)

The passage above proves the confusion about faith and works is not Biblical, but manmade. The confusion we see about works stems from coming to the Word with biases against works. In an attempt to stand against legalistic churches that give us the impression we can work our way into heaven, we are setting out to prove them wrong before we've ever even read a page of the Bible. This defensiveness makes us stick things in the Word that aren't in there, and create debates it never even addresses. Our works do not save us. Nowhere should this confusion even enter the picture. The Bible says that we are saved by grace through faith (Ephesians 2:8). The passage above is clearly about the relevance of works in one's faith life, not that works substitute for faith or save us. Bringing salvation into the debate about works muddles the water, and distorts from the purpose of what works really are. It also gives people the impression that works have no bearing on our faith, and that it doesn't matter what we do – because salvation is about faith.

Here and now, I am going to settle the faith vs. works debate. The issue is not faith against works, but the believer's call to faith and works. It doesn't mean that believers are saved by what they do, but that everything we do in this life should be a reflection of our salvation. The way we treat others, love our families, love our sisters and brothers in the church, carry ourselves, dress, and interact are all expressions of how we, as believers, show the world we've transformed from glory to glory and faith to faith. It matters what we believe, it matters what it does, and yes, it also matters whether or not people are able to connect the dots between the two.

Are you doing this stuff?

All throughout the Bible, we see the important connection between doing things with a right heart and motive and witnessing to other people. This is mentioned throughout because we can do things just to do them or with wrong motives. One of the most powerful passages about what we do and our witness is found in the very words of Jesus, Matthew 25:31-43:

"But when the Son of Man comes in His glory, and all the angels with Him, then He will sit on His glorious throne. All the nations will be gathered before Him; and He will separate

them from one another, as the shepherd separates the sheep from the goats; and He will put the sheep on His right, and the goats on the left.'

"Then the King will say to those on His right, 'Come, you who are blessed of My Father, inherit the kingdom prepared for you from the foundation of the world. For I was hungry, and you gave Me something to eat; I was thirsty, and you gave Me something to drink; I was a stranger, and you invited Me in; naked, and you clothed Me; I was sick, and you visited Me; I was in prison, and you came to Me.' Then the righteous will answer Him, 'Lord, when did we see You hungry, and feed You, or thirsty, and give You something to drink? And when did we see You a stranger, and invite You in, or naked, and clothe You? When did we see You sick, or in prison, and come to You?' The King will answer and say to them, 'Truly I say to you, to the extent that you did it to one of these brothers of Mine, even the least of them, you did it to Me.'

"Then He will also say to those on His left, 'Depart from Me, accursed ones, into the eternal fire which has been prepared for the devil and his angels; for I was hungry, and you gave Me nothing to eat; I was thirsty, and you gave Me nothing to drink; I was a stranger, and you did not invite Me in; naked, and you did not clothe Me; sick, and in prison, and you did not visit Me.' Then they themselves also will answer, 'Lord, when did we see You hungry, or thirsty, or a stranger, or naked, or sick, or in prison, and did not take care of You?' Then He will answer them, 'Truly I say to you, to the extent that you did not do it to one of the least of these, you did not do it to Me.' These will go away into eternal punishment, but the righteous into eternal life."

Jesus Himself tells us we need to do things for others out of our faith because as we do them, we are doing them for Him. We need to be proactive people who reach out to others. It is clearly not enough, even according to the Word, to just tell people about Jesus. We need to show people that Jesus cares about them by demonstrating attitudes of care and practicality in what we do. Let's also avoid the temptation to become excessively legalistic in an attempt to justify ourselves falsely and read these verses in an overly literal context. In examining the different directives Jesus provides in Matthew 25:31-43, we are able to now understand the following:

- **I was hungry, and you gave Me something to eat** – The human body has been designed to need food. In complete alignment with our physical need, God has provided us with plenty of natural resources in order to satisfy that physical need. As wickedness controls and prevails in our world, those natural resources – God's provision for humanity – has been usurped by evil people who desire to use natural instincts (such as threat of hunger or famine) to try and manipulate others. The world has, thus, become a dominance game of who controls who with the most resources. This mindset is contrary to God's Kingdom. I agree that the Word teaches we need to work for what we have (2 Thessalonians 3:10), but it's also wrong to expect people to work for wages that do not satisfy their most basic, primal needs.

  Seeing the hungry fed is intended here in a literal sense – that we should offer food to the hungry, providing proper food that represents health and good nutrition. This encompasses outreaches, food banks, meals with a "message" (that include a service or preaching afterward), and distribution of perfectly good food that would otherwise be wasted to those who are in need. It also represents standing for something deeper, as it recognizes the basic human need for individuals to have food. Believing that it is the Christian's duty to give food to the hungry means Christians should be opposed to political powers and programs that use starvation as a form of political control. It means believing in the promotion of a living wage, safe working conditions for workers, and the belief that people should be given the opportunity to provide for themselves and for their families without government interference.

It also means that we, as individuals, should be very well aware of how much we have and be willing to make a sacrifice every now and then so someone who doesn't have enough can have something. Whether you fast for world hunger and donate the money you would have spent on food or gain control of your own eating habits to avoid waste and gain control of your own body's process, making the effort to do the right thing when it comes to controlling food as a lust of the flesh is a witness to others.

- **I was thirsty, and you gave Me something to drink** – The body's composition is approximately seventy-five percent water. It only takes approximately three days for the body to dehydrate unto the point of death. This natural thirst is a type of the spiritual thirst each and every one of us has to discover the Living Water, which shall satisfy our spiritual longings (John 7:38). As we can understand this on a spiritual level, so too it is important to make sure we understand it practically. An individual without water or even access to clean drinking water is a person in trouble. Millions die annually due to unsanitary drinking conditions. Not having access to clean water also means people are unable to bathe, clean their clothes, cook their food, and do a host of other things we take for granted every day.

Being a Christian means providing liquid nourishment to the thirsty along with feeding those in need. This extends into the realm of any form of nourishment, including other non-alcoholic beverages beside water as available. It also means supporting various charitable efforts to maintain and provide clean drinking water, pumps, wells, and other systems to those who are in need of such.

- **I was a stranger, and you invited Me in** – Ancient culture prided itself upon hospitality. It was considered downright rude to reject strangers into one's home (Hebrews 13:2, 1 Peter 4:9) and provide them the basic foundations of shelter and nourishment for the duration of a visit. Being invited in as a stranger encompasses far more than just inviting someone over for a few minutes or asking someone to come over – it was about being responsible for someone's basic needs while they were away from home and in another person's care. The wording of the passage indicates the need to see to care and provision for others beyond our own family – thus eroding any principle of nepotism that tends to bind and blind in our world.

This is a basic principle of personal accountability for another life that is not a life we may consider ourselves responsible for on a regular basis. Any time someone is coming somewhere at our request, we become responsible for them. It is wrong to invite someone to something, claiming to host an event, and then not take care of them – especially if the minister is travelling to a region which they are unfamiliar with. This extends in church matters, especially when it comes to preachers and teachers who come in for an event. It is hospitable to see they are cared for in a hotel, with somewhere to rest, and given the best offering we can possibly give. It also extends to giving shelter to those who do not have any, such as the establishment and volunteer participation in a homeless shelter.

In a more general context, this applies to a willingness to extend our borders beyond those with whom we are most familiar and comfortable. It is easy to allow those we know to be a part of our inner circle and invite them to do things with us. It's a part of the Gospel to invite people to do things – to welcome in strangers – within our lives and our work. Yes, you can invite someone to go to church, but what about just being somebody's friend? Have a meal with them, talk to them, learn about them, love them as a human being – and stop treating them as if your only interest in them is a conversion agenda.

- **Naked, and you clothed Me** – Over the past several thousand years, clothing has become a social statement. We focus more on the social statements of clothing than we do practical elements, and we often forget that clothing has a practical purpose. Clothing is a form of shelter for the body against the elements of this world. Not having proper clothing can cause the body to become too hot or too cold, exposed to injury, or induce certain types of disease and illness. It's important that, as human beings, we have proper access to clothing that protects the body and preserves it from foreign invasion.

  Yes, we are commanded to clothe those who are physically naked, unable to provide practical clothing for themselves. Clothing drives, donations to organizations that give clothing away or who use money from clothing sales to provide for the needs of the poor, or to contribute to clothing projects that engage in Fair Trade practices, which help to profit those who are a part of underdeveloped work force cultures.

  Many cultures recognize nakedness or lack of clothing as a source of shame, and use nakedness as an image of shame or violation. This verse also reminds us, by extension, to help, protect, and encourage those who have been violated or shamed (such as rape, sexual abuse, violence, discrimination, or mistreatment).

- **I was sick, and you visited Me** – Today we have hospitals, doctors, and nursing homes to care for the sick. In ancient times, the scenario was not so. The sick were regarded as being plagued for some sort of wrongdoing or somehow under a spiritual curse, and often considered untouchable. People were afraid that every disease would spread or "catch" with no more than nominal contact. The sick were also regarded as a burden on families because they were unable to work and earn their keep in agricultural and merchant-based societies. This meant chronic illness was cause for isolation and loneliness, not to mention a sick individual being rejected by their families and forced to a life of begging and poverty.

The command to visit the sick was a ministry of healing, all in itself. It recognizes the human element in healing, the basic need each human being has to interact with others in a compassionate and empathetic way. Today we can understand this as a need to visit the elderly, shut-ins, chronically ill in hospitals and nursing homes, and even make a point to reach out to hospital patients. It also reminds us of the need to make ourselves available to others when someone is sick, whether temporarily or terminally. Bringing food or a gift, making a visit to help with laundry, cooking, or cleaning, or letting someone know you are thinking of them is vital to cure the wound of loneliness.

- **I was in prison, and you came to Me** – When I lived in the Midwest, people treated the county jail as if it was the hotspot for ministry opportunity. Between all the local ministers, over thirty-five services per week were held in that tiny local jail. Out of all the places I have lived, that was the only one where I saw such a response to prison ministry. Most of the time, prison ministry is treated here as it is in many other parts of the world – a non-existent, unimportant aspect to ministry life.

People tend to assume inmates deserve to be in prison, and have done something so unpardonable and unforgivable that they deserve whatever treatment they receive. Historically speaking, prisoners have been regarded as the lowest of the low. Ancient prisons were filled with representations of political sieges (prisoners of war), individuals guilty of theft, unable to pay their debts, or guilty of other crimes, including religious confessions contrary to a society's custom. Prisons were unsanitary, dangerous places, and inmates faced torture, violence, and brutal deaths.

So why would Jesus encourage us, as believers, to visit those in prison? Let us never forget Jesus Himself was tried and convicted as a criminal, and was not guilty of any crime (John 18:38, Luke 23:4). We need to stop assuming that everyone in prison is guilty of the crime society has convicted them of. Not everyone who goes to jail is, in fact, guilty. Not everyone who is in prison is indignant to the crimes they have committed, nor is everyone in prison a repeat offender. Sometimes things happen, circumstances are mitigating, and people are forced into situations which we could never imagine what we would do had we been in that same situation.

Visiting inmates in prison is a humbling experience. It reminds us that we are all sinners, and but for the grace of God are we where we are today. Through visiting prisoners, God wants us to remember those who are legally bound to a justice system that is not always just, whether they are there of their own doing, or not. God wants people to realize forgiveness exists, no matter the circumstances behind an offense.

By extension, we are to remember those who are imprisoned by any host of issues, problems, or situations that keep them bound. As Christians, we are called to proclaim freedom to the captives (Isaiah 61:1). Whether a person is bound by the law (imprisonment) or by physical, emotional, mental, or addictive issues, we are still called to reach out to them, offering them a true liberty and a true Christian love.

All the things listed here are practical, everyday things rather than deeply spiritual actions. We need to resist the temptation to assess everything from a spiritual perspective and to assume every spiritual need has a deep, ethereal cause. It's easy to think that we're "feeding" people the Word through teaching CDs and YouTube videos, and ignore other more practical needs people have. Evangelism is a spiritual process and purpose, but don't get so caught up in the spiritual that you ignore the natural. Someone can't focus on receiving the Word of the Lord if they are so hungry, it is the ultimate focal point of their lives. Some people can't receive the Gospel until they receive a practical need met. We need to stop assuming that every need will be met by some extraordinary power and realize the answer to every problem is not a Bible verse, to tell someone you are going to pray for them (when you really won't), or patting someone on the back and telling them everything will be all right. Being a Christian and daring to be a witness for Christ means living our faith. We live our faith by standing for, believing in, and conducting ourselves in ways that bring about a whole sense of promise and justice to people's lives. It's not just about going to church on Sunday and Bible study on Wednesdays. If the Word that we hear when we are in church is not changing who we are as people, we are going to be ineffective Christians and extremely poor witnesses of our faith.

Another relevant point: leave the politics out of your effective works. I understand that in order to start a homeless shelter or work in prison ministry, you sometimes have to deal with political channels and follow secular rules. Telling people who to vote for, hoping a candidate will ensure your rights, or launching an all-out war for a political cause is not the sort of work that brings in a witness. Politics are a belligerent and hostile game, and it is not effective witnessing to spend your time focusing on politics. Every one of us is entitled to an opinion about secular matters, but those matters should not mix with nor override our position as Kingdom citizens. Do something for someone instead of doing something for the government.

Who are you doing these things unto?

Now we get to the fun part of doing the right things for others: motives. Some of the most active, involved, and visible volunteers have the most self-centered motives. People do good things for all sorts of reasons: to get noticed, for publicity, to look good, to get close to someone who also does the work and seems important, to get out of legal trouble, to fulfill a program or course requirement, or because someone else told them they had to do it. All of the reasons I just mentioned indicates someone is doing one of these things "unto" someone other than the Lord.

An example of this is the behind-the-scenes truth of ministry today. It is almost impossible to get individuals to volunteer for ministry assistance. It's fine to expect the minister to work for next to nothing, not even an offering at times, but people who do work as assistants, armor bearers, and technical assistants almost always expect to be paid for their time and work. I do not think there is anything wrong with compensating people for their time and work, especially if the ministry is able to afford it. The expectation that people think they should be compensated for church work, however, truly bothers me. If someone is a part of the ministry and has a skill that can benefit the work of that ministry, that skill should be offered to further the Kingdom work present in that ministry.

The same logic is true when it comes to evangelization. I fully well recognize that people have expenses and we have bills that need to be paid. I do not suggest that you do everything for free in your life, nor that people should be allowed to take advantage of you. How many of us, however, are guilty of throwing the good that we do in someone else's face when we don't feel they responded as they should? How many of us have used the opportunity to do something good to advance ourselves or something we're doing? Have you ever stopped to think about how this kind of behavior might negatively affect your evangelical witness? If we want evangelism to be effective, we need to stop doing things just to get by, get noticed, or meet expectations. Every action, every good work, everything we do must be an extension of our love for God, a visible display of our faith. It should not be about anything except doing it unto the Lord, and doing it unto His service. Doing something to make the moment about you equates to a misrepresentation of the Gospel.

The company we keep

Think for a few minutes about who your "Christian" friends are. Do your friends echo the attitudes you have about the Gospel and evangelization? I'm not asking if your friends go to church, or if they don't watch television, or how often they study the Bible...do they claim to live the beliefs you espouse? Do they live within the bounds of guidelines by which you yourself ascribe?

Over my years as a Christian leader, I find that it's not uncommon for believers to espouse other individuals who claim to be believers as their friends, without any idea as to what they really believe and how they really live. Sure, they may think as long as they claim to believe in a specific doctrine or agree on some social issue, they are a good choice for a friend. They do not, however, consider how this person feels about other issues or how this friend's influence in their lives could affect how a non-believer might respond to their association with this other individual.

Sure, nobody agrees with anyone else one hundred percent of the time. We are all subject to disagreements, and it's expected that not every disagreement should lead to the dissolution of a friendship or relationship. Part of being human is learning to agree to disagree, and picking and choosing the things that are 'deal breakers' is a part of that process. I think it's worth examining, however, just what our "deal breakers" are and whether or not the company we keep is hampering our own witness to others.

Whether right or wrong, people judge us by our associations. We are keenly judged and assessed by the beliefs and feelings of others around us. If someone among us has a certain attitude, behavior, or belief about something and is particularly vocal about it, others will assume we have the same viewpoint, unless we are somehow outspoken about our position. Even then, it is very possible someone will not want to speak with us because we choose to associate with someone who feels a way that is considered a personal assault or threat toward them.

I am not suggesting you get rid of all your friends who disagree with you about things, even if they are controversial issues. I would encourage you, however, to look at how those who claim to be Christians are making you appear, especially if you don't agree with their viewpoints. It's important that we assess our friends by more than just one or two issues, or more than just where they go to church. If you are a Christian, your Christian friends should uphold the majors of love and good conduct. There are some things that Christians should never partake in. Things like excessive alcohol abuse or recreational drug use, and hate speech and actions are never acceptable. "My friend does it!" is not accountable conduct, and taints a negative shadow on the Gospel.

We also need to pay careful attention to those who are our leaders, those who have authority over us, the ministries of which we are a part of, and those who influence us in our faith. If we are a part of a ministry that is proclaiming a certain belief system or attitude we are opposed to, or we have a leader that is doing the same, we need to assess our role with such people and in such a position, and take the matter before the Lord for action and repositioning.

Having friends that are non-believers

There are some leaders who believe it's wrong to have friends, especially close friendships, with people who are not believers. I strongly disagree with this perspective. As Christians, we are called to impact the world. We can't impact the world if we can't get along with anybody in it, and we need to separate the concept of the world from our ideas about people. People may be a part of the world, but they are still an individual, with their own thoughts, feelings, and opinions. We don't like it when the world stereotypes Christians and makes us all out to be the same as a few very vocal individuals who ruin it for the rest of us. Well, people in the world don't like to be stereotyped as having the same thoughts and feelings as the world's noise makers, either. Getting to know people, learn about people, and like people for who they are goes a long way in Kingdom understanding and purpose.

Favor with God...and men

And Jesus kept increasing in wisdom and stature, and in favor with God and men. (Luke 2:52).

We've all heard the verse, *"You adulteresses, do you not know that friendship with the world is hostility toward God? Therefore whoever wishes to be a friend of the world makes himself an enemy of God."* (James 4:4) This verse is often invoked in the concept of a world attitude and of worldly success. People who are deemed successful in a world view are often considered to be "friends of the world" and therefore, "enemies with God." This either-or proposition causes Christians to feel guilty for success, for having an impact that transcends beyond the church, and for having friends who are not Christian.

We often complain about the impact the world is having on the church, but do we stop to realize that we also complain about the impact Christians have on the world? Sometimes I feel leaders in the church give the message that Christians should do nothing but attend church. If people are visible representatives of productivity and aspiration, they are condemned as not being "Christian" enough, having been tainted by the world. If Christians do not have aspirations, they are branded as being of negative witness.

This madness must stop because Christians should be visible representatives of their faith in various places, not just the church. Not everyone is called to be in five-fold ministry, be a preacher, or work in full-time ministry. This notion that everyone is called to full-time ministry must stop because people need to be free to fulfill what God has called them to be. Some people are fabulous businessmen and women, some are fabulous teachers, some doctors, some lawyers, some housekeepers, and some a variety of other things that are just as needed and important in this world. Devaluing such work devalues the principle of being living witnesses, sent into every aspect of life to bring with us the witness of

Christ.

I do not question there is more than one way to be successful, and that worldly success is not necessarily the measure of success or aspiration in our lives. Certainly we, as Christians, must find balance and avoid becoming excessively materialistic or preoccupied with money. At the same time, Christians should be an excellent people, noted for doing a good job, and noted by their excellent conduct, job performance, and work quality that we find favor with people in the world. This comes about as we work hard, make ourselves pleasant and polite, and carry ourselves with self-respect. It also means we extend respect to those around us and those in authority, whether we like or agree with them. The Word tells us that Jesus Himself grew, and gained favor with God and with man. We do not impact the world if we do not have favor with people. If we are living epistles, being read of all men, being productive and successful people is part of that. People can tell when you are doing something genuinely well, and when you are doing something to just get by.

As Christians, we should find favor everywhere we go because of how we conduct ourselves. Does this always happen? No, but it should happen enough of the time that people wonder what is different about you and how they too can have whatever it is that you have.

CHAPTER SEVEN

HOLINESS AND EVANGELISM

The Bible is very easy to understand. But we Christians are a bunch
of scheming swindlers. We pretend to be unable to understand
it because we know very well that the minute we understand,
we are obliged to act accordingly.
- Soren Kierkegaard[1]

Holiness is a big word in many Christian circles today. In an attempt to redefine the more traditional understandings of holiness, holiness has become a term used to correct social behaviors deemed wrong or unseemly. This concept of "holiness" has become a new means of evangelization in many circles and is also the seat of social and political activism against certain behaviors and lifestyles. We could define this as an attempt to force people into our concept of holiness, attempting to make people see Christianity is right via social persuasion rather than true witnessing with the Gospel of Christ.

As a result of the holiness push, people are more at odds than they have ever been in years prior. Family members are at odds over personal and lifestyle choices and it is more difficult than ever to maintain friends. The church itself is at odds over many of these issues, unsure of how to regulate and interact with one another – let alone how to handle the issue of holiness with the real world.

It's probably safe to say that forcing people into holiness has been one of the most ineffective means in evangelism history. So where did the emphasis on "holiness" come from – and is this what God had in mind when he commanded His people to be holy? Do we understand holiness? How does holiness pertain to evangelism?

Understanding the history of "holiness"

"Holiness" as we understand it today comes from an American evangelical movement stemming from social codes and understanding as relates to conversion and revival movements in the 1800s. The Holiness Movement has its origins in Methodism (known best for the Methodist Church), a group which emphasized the ability to live free from sin if one would improve or change personal conduct. This means a lot of what came out of this movement was regulation and legislation of personal conducts. It was believed that one was sanctified as an entire being, and that is what made one able to live a holy – and eventually, sinless – life.

Prior to the 1800s, holiness was not the focus of the majority of denominations - doctrine was. Protestant movements were far more into trying to fit the Word into their doctrine than how to live one's faith. Christians of old were just as superstitious, common, and integrated with modern society as non-believers were. The exception to this was Calvinism, which was known for its austere codes of conduct - but the reality of Calvinist descendants was that they behaved often quite common and quite raucous as others did, despite the so-called "conducts" of their system. The Pilgrims, for example, landed at Plymouth Rock in Massachusetts because they ran out of beer, as is documented on their landing site. So what was it about this time frame that spawned such a radical movement steeped in examination of personal conduct? The 1700s and 1800s represented mass change in ideas and concepts among most classes of society. With changing times came changing approaches to what was truly important in the life of a believer, and in how the life of a believer was defined. Advances in science and medicine, transportation, world events, clothing, and politics, and revolution spawned vices: alcohol, gambling, smoking, saloons, and prostitution. Enter the holiness movement, which sought to put a stop to vices that were perceived as destroying the family, the nation, and by extension, the church.

The Holiness Movement's most profound impact was its vast and extensive number of "holiness codes," which are still in place in one form or another in various denominations today. These did not exist before the success of the Holiness Movement, and, in many ways, have relaxed over the decades since. The codes we have come to associate with Holiness denominations - no smoking, no drinking, no dancing, no gambling, no hair-cutting for women, no long hair for men, long pants for men, no pants for women, no make-up, and many other beliefs, several of which people would write off as absurd today. Holiness codes were a response to changing times, changing fashions, changing attitudes - in short, they were a response to change. They were a bit more equal between the sexes than we proclaim today, but not much. For example: men were forbidden to wear any sort of jewelry, they had to wear long sleeves, and neck ties were considered "adornment." There were those who believed it was impossible to even be saved if you lived in a city, believing the urban environment to be cause for sin and debauchery. Many also believed that "holiness" translated to segregation of blacks and whites, and considered such integration to be appalling, a disrespect to God and His "separation" of the races.

Clearly, the translation of "holiness" for people in this time frame was a reaction to a changing culture, of which they disapproved. The first women's liberation movement in American history was the Suffragist Movement, in full swing during this era; abolitionism and the push to end slavery was also causing a changing course of time, and an integration of former slaves into society; the invention of the bicycle caused fashion to change, especially for women; temperance (the movement to abolish alcohol) was prominent among Baptist and Methodist churches in the United States; as was a general health movement, pushing people to depart from cities, believing air and poor nutrition were to blame for a host of ailments, much of their theories based upon "junk science."

Having said all of that, what we associate with "holiness" today comes from these associated movements, not from a true Biblical understanding of what it means to be holy. They are traditions, passed down for the past three hundred or so years - and sometimes, even less than that - about what is to define the "exterior" of a believer. We do not even uphold all of these codes today. Most people, thankfully, have abandoned the racism prevalent in the Holiness and Methodist Movements (although, unfortunately, it is not completely gone). No one would assume you can't be saved if you live in a city, and men are not forced to wear long pants, long sleeves, and never wear a neck tie. We have not, however, abandoned the holiness codes for women. Women are still chastised for wearing cute shoes, a skirt that is above the ankles, cutting hair, wearing make-up, or wearing short sleeves, in many circles. And, as we can see from current events - they are also still assessed by their clothing, by individual standards of the holiness code.

To some, a movement with a bunch of rules from the 1800s may not seem to have a lot of relevance in evangelism today, but it does – perhaps more than you can imagine. The Holiness Movement and its associated codes marked a change in the way people viewed evangelism, conversion, and sanctification. Instead of viewing conversion as an inward change that extends outward, holiness codes called attention to outward behaviors viewed as sinful, and the call to change those. In other words: it turned evangelism into a systematic attack on people and outward behaviors rather than working to change the inner man via the power of the Holy Spirit. It also means that the inward, or spiritual, work of a person was not the focus – correcting behaviors that were deemed "unacceptable" were the focus. Conversion was seen as halting these behaviors – nothing more, nothing less.

There are a lot of reasons why such a mentality becomes problematic. The first is that people quickly and easily learned how to cheat the system and go on doing whatever it was they were doing prior, because they felt salvation came down to maintaining codes rather than walking with the Lord. As long as a skirt was long enough, a shirt's sleeves were long enough, hair was the right length, and nobody was drinking or smoking...you could slide by with getting into heaven, no matter what else you were doing. The second is that salvation becomes marked as a one-time event, not a daily continuing process as we walk toward the mark the Lord has set for us. It sets us on the path of following human rules rather than discovering God's principles for us; that we can "get by" if we keep up these ideals and principles. Perhaps the most problematic of all mentalities in such thinking, however, is that the assorted list of holiness rules are the varied things by which believers are defined. If someone can start adapting the rules – that means they have been transformed.

This is how evangelism most often takes shape today: we want people to "look" the part. If we can get them to look right, sound right, and act according to our rules, then we've accomplished something. Evangelism today is, in many ways, a superficial system: we think if someone appears to have abandoned something we deem problematic, that we've done our job. Evangelism was never intended to have a showmanship approach; it was the beginning to discipleship. It does not end at an altar call or when someone adopts a certain style of dress or lifestyle change. People today run around, trying to tell non-believers that their conduct is "unholy" or "against the Bible" in the hopes that they will drop their conducts and abandon their actions that are not in alignment with modern-day holiness codes. The results are arguments, fights, and quarrels with people as non-believers attempt to defend a character assault, whether or not it is justified. Instead of starting a discussion on something spiritual, everything is about what is immediately seen or perceived – judgments, pure and simple.

No wonder "evangelistic" efforts are so unsuccessful. How do you feel when you are judged on the spot by someone else's standards? And we, as a church, cannot even say in good conscience that many of these teachings based on the holiness codes are even Biblical; they were social prohibitions in many instances, plain and simple. Trying to impose these on the world has been a failure of every imagination. Rather than produce fruit unto repentance, holiness codes have caused believers to be more self-righteous than ever – and more distant from the needs and concerns of those who need to hear the Gospel.

Transferring the burden of holiness to the non-believer

The Bible tells us that God's people were to be "holy" and "set apart," which is what "holy" means. The term "holy" or "holiness," which is the state of being set apart, was first used to describe the Hebrews and their differences from the tribes around them. Because God called them, gave them His law, and established them as His own people, they were not to believe, behave, live, or practice as the nations around them. The laws which often seem arbitrary or outlandish to us today were all distinguishing marks that these people had been selected by God and were, therefore, different from all others around them.

We know from Biblical history that the law written in stone did not change as many people's hearts as one might have hoped. Down the ages, the people of Israel fell time and time again into the idolatries and sins of the people around them. The reason for this is simple: the law alone was not enough to change the hearts of people. Following exterior rules and codes was not enough to make people different. While it might have helped establish order within the group, it would only be a matter of time before someone fell, and the whole nation often followed.

Are we noticing a trend? Does any of this sound familiar? How many people do you know in church who don't live up to their own doctrinal "holiness codes?" How many do you know who condemn others for one sin, but commit several others in that one's place. How many are trying to live up to the law, without having undergone internal transformation?

Nobody in history was ever saved unto holiness by following rules. Nobody in history was ever saved because of the influences of the non-believer. Jesus Christ entered the picture because God knew our best efforts to try and do right by God would eventually end the same way. Without the grace of God working in an individual, every one of us can try to achieve perfect conduct and fail every single time. We can be "set apart" now for God because of the internal work Jesus Christ does within us, but there remains an order to holiness. Jesus Christ must first be a part of our lives, and be transforming us within for us to be holy in our exterior walk. Our best efforts to be saved by following a laundry list will leave us exhausted...and lost.

Today we expect the non-believer to uphold our laundry list of "codes" when we don't even follow them ourselves. Instead of living up to our own standards, we expect the world to follow them. When the world doesn't follow them, we use it as a means to condemn and insult them. This is contrary to the purpose of holiness; it is contrary as to what it is supposed to mean to be holy and to walk in holiness; and it also proves that God's so-called people aren't holy themselves. Holiness was never meant to be an excuse to offend nor attack others.

Holiness and evangelism

If I were to summarize the role holiness plays in evangelism, it is that your holiness should speak for itself in your own conduct when you are witnessing to someone else. As stated above, the word "holy" simply means "set apart for a purpose." "Holiness," therefore, refers to the state or condition of being set apart for a purpose. In other words: holiness is not a lifestyle, it is not a code, it is not a list of exterior rules - it is a condition, it is a state, it is a way of being. Holiness is something we become as Christ has transformed us, and it becomes something that we are. It is not something we can adopt by a long list of do's and don'ts created to counter-culture believers and avoid change.

So, in short, holiness is for believers. We should be modeling the things we claim to believe and following the precepts we claim to adhere to. We should be echoing the love of God while reflecting the beliefs and precepts we say we believe in. In short – holiness should be something seen in evangelism, not pounded over the heads of the non-believers that we reach out to.

Why is this? Because holiness as an evangelistic weapon

renders evangelism ineffective. It takes holiness, which is a good and powerful marker of God's people, and turns it into a nasty weapon, used to demean people. This is not what holiness is about, nor is it a proper exercise thereof. The proper exercise of holiness is to understand it to a point where you are able to live it and display that, causing people to recognize and see that God has done a work within you and it has changed you.

Is John the Baptist a model of evangelism?

When people argue for holiness in evangelism, people tend to defend their methods and positions via John the Baptist. Is this an accurate assessment of John's preaching? Is John the Baptist the ultimate answer as to why we should "evangelize hard"...or are we missing something in John's work and purpose?

Now in those days John the Baptist came, preaching in the wilderness of Judea, saying, "Repent, for the kingdom of heaven is at hand." For this is the one referred to by Isaiah the prophet when he said, "THE VOICE OF ONE CRYING IN THE WILDERNESS, 'MAKE READY THE WAY OF THE LORD, MAKE HIS PATHS STRAIGHT!'"

Now John himself had a garment of camel's hair and a leather belt around his waist; and his food was locusts and wild honey. Then Jerusalem was going out to him, and all Judea and all the district around the Jordan; and they were being baptized by him in the Jordan River, as they confessed their sins.

But when he saw many of the Pharisees and Sadducees coming for baptism, he said to them, "You brood of vipers, who warned you to flee from the wrath to come? Therefore bear fruit in keeping with repentance; and do not suppose that you can say to yourselves, 'We have Abraham for our father'; for I say to you that from these stones God is able to raise up children to Abraham. The axe is already laid at the root of the trees; therefore every tree that does not bear good fruit is cut down and thrown into the fire.

"As for me, I baptize you with water for repentance, but He who is coming after me is mightier than I, and I am not fit to remove His sandals; He will baptize you with the Holy Spirit and fire. His winnowing fork is in His hand, and He will thoroughly clear His threshing floor; and He will gather His wheat into the barn, but He will burn up the chaff with unquenchable fire." (Matthew 3:1-11)

I think the first thing we need to realize is that the Bible never anywhere describes John as an "evangelist." The Bible says John the Baptist went preaching and baptizing as a forerunner for the work of Jesus. According to the time in which John lived, he would have been classified as a prophet, because he lived prior to the time of the five-fold ministry. In the work and personality of John, there is nothing to suggest the characters of an evangelist. He proclaimed and prepared the hearts of people for the coming of Christ, but his typology is much closer to that of an apostle rather than an evangelist. The people John directly addressed (leaders of the Jewish people) is in keeping with the work and character of the apostle rather than an evangelist. John's address of the leaders reveals that his work was directed more towards people who already believed in God, at least somewhat, and had some knowledge of Him through their teachings and traditions. His call was not to the non-believer, but to those who already (sort-of) believed. These were the people who were aware of the law and times from the law to watch for the Messiah, and needed to be the people who were prepared to represent Him and His coming to the world. The nature of his teaching, therefore, was stronger than that of an evangelist dealing strictly with non-believers. John dealt with people who knew better, but did not do better.

The preaching of John the Baptist was strong, no doubt. It was strong for a reason. This does not mean we should preach in such a strong manner at all times, or that this is the "model" for work with non-believers. On the contrary, it is a clear address to those who know better (who have enough knowledge of the Word to know how to act), but don't. It is a word not addressing non-believers, but rather...so-called believers.

John the Baptist is not talking to your unsaved friend, he's talking to you. I believe if the church could just grasp hold of this, they would become far better witnesses to the Gospel.

Do not do what you hate

The Gospel of Thomas is a controversial document, no doubt. If we can separate ourselves from the controversy for a bit, however, we can learn a very important precept as relates to holiness and evangelism in one of its passages. The Gospel of Thomas, verses 5 and 6, read:

Jesus said, "Recognize what is in your sight, and that which is hidden from you will become plain to you. For there is nothing hidden which will not become manifest."

His disciples questioned him and said to him, "Do you want us to fast? How shall we pray? Shall we give alms? What diet shall we observe?"

Jesus said, "Do not tell lies, and do not do what you hate, for all things are plain in the sight of heaven. For nothing hidden will not become manifest, and nothing covered will remain without being uncovered." [2]

Both verses 5 and 6 connect, but the bottom line I think of both of them in summary is: stop looking for something that's not so obvious. In other words: stop being so deep all the time. The church today likes to be "deep," give "deep answers," and, in general, sound much smarter than we are. Sometimes we are "deeping" ourselves right out of relevance. We can try so hard to find deep things, hidden things, secret things, that we miss what's right in front of us. If someone is standing in front of you, seriously in need of something, they don't need some big, deep, theological answer to solve their problems. There is no reason to stand there and tell them the Lord will provide for all their needs if you can do it. If there is some way you can meet the immediate need they have, you need to step up and meet it. Recognize that which is plain, and the deeper meanings of things will be manifest to you. Stop looking for deep answers, and start looking for practical ways to reach out.

114

I like verse six in *The Gospel of Thomas* because it takes the complicated out of holiness and, in essence, out of following Jesus. We believers like to make things so complicated. I think that somewhere in our minds we think that if we make things as complicated as possible, that will somehow get us closer to Jesus. If it's confusing, that makes it "deep" and hard to follow...and then only a few people can really understand it. It doesn't get us closer, it just creates confusion and mess. Jesus didn't ask us to do half the things we pursue in His Name. He never told us we had to stop watching television, give up our cell phones, stop eating chocolate, or act in a generally disgruntled manner. What we need to do is stop giving things up and making random sacrifices for no reason when our witness relies on our ability to be honest and stop chasing after things we hate. If we claim to be opposed to it, we shouldn't be doing it. Living lives of hypocrisy are far more detrimental to our witness to the world than watching a television show or listening to the radio. We need to stop thinking adherence to many made-up rules will make us look holy, and start living by the principles we know really exist.

This also means that the endless scandals in the church are also quite detrimental to witnessing – whether we are the ones who are personally guilty of the infractions, or not. When big-name preachers live however they please, with no consideration as to how this will affect their witness, it helps people justify their own behaviors and their own sins. When church matters arise internally, they must be dealt with internally. Yes, we must forgive sins, but we must also consider how such behaviors affect the entire Body. Sitting a leader down who has engaged in something they are supposed to "hate" is not unforgiveness, it is doing what is best for the entire Body. It is making sure we have a consistent witness and we are not claiming one thing and then condoning another.

Such incidents should call to mind our own consistencies in claim. We're big to jump on the finger-pointing bandwagon when something big comes up, but God notices small things, too! Sometimes those small things are just as bad (if not worse) than the "big things." If you acknowledge God is against certain things, such as gossip or tale-bearing, then you shouldn't be doing these things.

Babies n' bullies

When children are young, they have not developed to a point where they have a comprehensive understanding of empathy or feeling for others. We've all seen toddlers who take other children's toys, throw fits and tantrums, and seem to sing the singular song of "ME, ME, ME, ME, ME!" Parents speak of what a difficult age the "terrible twos" are, having to watch their children every minute and keep a careful cap on their behaviors. They deal with crying, screaming fits, kicking and hitting, and sometimes even biting. The experience is exhausting for parents, who report being so grateful when the experience passes. Once it does, children are taught how to share, how to get along with others, and are encouraged to think about other people, beside what they may see, feel, think, or want.

No parent in their right mind desires their child to remain in the state of the "terrible twos." Most parents would also agree that seeing their children grow up to maturity is a good thing. Changing diapers, having to prepare formula, and having to constantly regulate very young children are all tasks that grow tiresome after awhile. We understand this precept in the natural realm. A child who was still wearing diapers, drinking formula, and throwing tantrums when they are ten years old would be considered a problem, not a socialized part of life. Selfish children are not considered desirable friends or playmates, and efforts to socialize them are taken within the bounds of appropriate understanding. These children become bullies when their behavior is left unchecked. So if we understand and nod our heads about this in the natural...why do we tolerate, even encourage such in the spiritual?

On a spiritual level, the church today is nursing along a general sense of immaturity among its people. We don't want to hear it, but it's the truth. We are witnessing a church full of tantrum-throwing adults who are mad at God because they didn't get their own way, or are using past hurts and offenses generated from church members (sometimes justified, sometimes not) to fuel this immature state of being. Because the church has bred members to be preoccupied with themselves, the church is simply not doing its job. It has become a matter of "I am over here, and I am right" (thus leading to spiritual bullying), whether or not such is even valid or useful.

A church preoccupied with its own selfishness is a church full of babies. A church trying to witness in this state becomes a church of bullies. The result equates to lacking faith and completely ineffective evangelism.

You can get mad at me for what I just said, or you can acknowledge that it is true, and we can start to rectify the problem. Today's church flocks to teaching that does not challenge it to grow or mature. We hear more about gaining material things and being set financially than we do about obtaining spiritual principles and seeing things from an eternal perspective. This has led to a pervasive attitude of justified selfishness among many, and a negative witness among many more. Instead of genuinely reaching out and acting like they care about others, they are all about one singular agenda...themselves.

A selfish church is a trite church. It's when we are simply waiting for someone else to shut up so we can do all the talking, when we stop listening to the things people are trying to tell us because we aren't really interested, and when we think everything in the world can be resolved by spouting off a Bible verse and a little cute "positive thinking" phrase. Acting like this – telling people, "Oh, I'll pray for you!" when we can really do something concrete to help them, brushing people's problems off, and ignoring the genuine opportunity to reach out to someone else – gives people the message that God doesn't care about their issues, either.

It also leads to severe misunderstanding in the right and wrong ways to approach people in evangelism. It's the easy way out to think we will shame people into accepting the Gospel because it doesn't require any effort or time. It takes a lot more time to talk to someone and reach them where they are...and too many Christians are too busy, too preoccupied, and too self-absorbed to take the time to do this.

We can't throw endless tantrums and expect people to want what we have to offer spiritually. We can't handle spiritual matters as if everyone, including us, is stupid and hope they will take the bait. We can't attempt to bully people into the Gospel and think it's going to fly. These have been the methods used for many years in our modern times and they are simply not working.

We need to formulate a new-old plan. It's new because we're not doing it in recorded memory (it's new for us), but it's old because it goes back to Biblical wisdom. Stop using a misguided sense of Biblical knowledge, holiness, or plain immaturity as excuses not to reach out at all or not reach out properly.

If you walk away with nothing else from this book, I pray you walk away with the realization that the Bible addresses different people at different times and we cannot apply every single verse to every single situation or application. At times, the Word was speaking to believers, at times, it was addressing issues pertinent to non-believers, at other times, it was addressing leaders, at other times, general non-ordained church members, and still at other times, there were words for specified groups of people, such as government officials, husbands, wives, children, slaves, or merchants. This means not every word written in the Bible is for every single person to apply literally to themselves. Given I am not a government official, God's words to government officials may be beneficial in a general sense to me, but I am not going to be able to apply it in the exact way it was written.

Expecting the unsaved to adhere to Biblical holiness (or, maybe better put, our concept of Biblical holiness) is not a method of salvation. On the contrary, the Word gives us an interesting command about maturity that, clearly being for the church, is something that can help us with our evangelistic witness if we will allow it:

Concerning him we have much to say, and it is hard to explain, since you have become dull of hearing. For though by this time you ought to be teachers, you have need again for someone to teach you the elementary principles of the

118

oracles of God, and you have come to need milk and not solid food. For everyone who partakes only of milk is not accustomed to the word of righteousness, for he is an infant. But solid food is for the mature, who because of practice have their senses trained to discern good and evil.

Therefore leaving the elementary teaching about the Christ, let us press on to maturity, not laying again a foundation of repentance from dead works and of faith toward God, of instruction about washings and laying on of hands, and the resurrection of the dead and eternal judgment. And this we will do, if God permits. (Hebrews 5:11-6:3)

Now, many people use this passage to speak of difficulty when evangelizing non-believers. People complain that outsiders are simply unwilling to accept what believers have to say and are unwilling to listen. This may be true, but whose attitude do we need to look at here? If we understand the verse in its context, it's talking about just that kind of attitude: people who are so immature in their faith, they cannot understand anything beyond the barest of the basics. The problem, however, is that this passage is clearly speaking about people in the church; it is not talking about non-believers or discussing with non-believers. It is describing a church that has grown so preoccupied with itself and with whatever it deems most relevant, most important, and most desirable, it is rejecting the deeper teachings and, as a result, is swallowing up everything whole that comes along to entertain it.

Natural babies and natural toddlers don't live in a discerning point in their lives. They recognize those who are closest to them, but they don't have the world awareness to know who will bring them good or harm; they simply trust everyone that comes along to give them whatever it is they think they need. The same is what happens when we have an immature church: people gravitate from person to person, leader to leader, with no discipline or awareness needed for proper discernment. Instead of being able to reach outward, immature church members are forever looking inward, trying to generate things for themselves.

The Bible clearly discourages believers from remaining immature in their faith. We should move past arguments about basic tenets of faith and move on to deeper matters that help believers apply the Word in practical ways. When we are mature and discerning, we can better understand just what we believe and how we can reach out with what we believe to meet and help other people. Staying in an immature state doesn't lead to a proper witness of the faith...it leads to babying and bullying.

Mature believers make the best witnesses, for one simple reason: they aren't preoccupied with themselves. Think about it for a minute: how many people do you know who are able to put themselves aside and reach out to other believers with the Gospel? Most of the time, we hear people asking for prayers that relate to their own needs and wants (finances, bigger ministries, material goods, etc.). Very seldom do we hear people pray that God will be able to use them in a better way to witness to others. This means if we want to evangelize better and have people come to church more frequently, we need to be people who stop teaching the same "basics" over and over again, and start teaching things that will help people have a better sense of God in their lives.

Correcting behaviors

I do believe that attempts to change the behavior of others through evangelism isn't so much about holiness or helping others as it is about control. The world today is a constant reminder that we don't live in Mayberry anymore (and, if you study history, you will find out we never did). Gone are the days of cozy families with twenty-three children behind a white picket fence. We live in a world that is much more diverse, with a whole host of ideas about how one can – and often does – live life. A variety of ideas means that the simplistic values many had either don't apply or cannot apply in the same way they used to. In the face of change comes the facet of control: there are many who want the world they remember back, even if getting it back is completely impossible.

This doesn't mean that the concepts or values people

have are necessarily incorrect; it simply means we must apply them in a context. If someone is genuinely doing something that is keeping them from God, that person should be informed so they can correct whatever it is they are doing. It is just a matter of how we do that.

The Apostle Paul had a definitive way of looking at the world, which we will discuss a little more in the next chapter. The apostle's powerful worldview was to see the work of Christ and the impact of God's grace upon all of humanity, because he saw God reaching out to all people through Christ. Most of what we see in the New Testament, however, is the apostle's church view: examining the different ways the church was excelling or failing. He praised the first, and corrected the second. From his work, we see the proper way to handle correction.

The Apostle Paul's letters were to the church, not the world. This means the way he addressed matters of correction were much bolder and more forceful than the ways in which he addressed public crowds of non-believers. He was forceful for one reason: those who were doing wrong knew they weren't supposed to be doing it. They had enough teaching and training to know better. They had, most likely, already been instructed privately and disciplined, but still insisted on behaving like they were. As a result, the Apostle Paul didn't waste a lot of time going over what they already knew what was wrong – he called it out, he was direct, and prayed for their restoration.

We need to be careful about imposing our belief systems upon non-believers. Our job is to preach Christ unto them, and to bring them to a point where they want to come into fellowship with God and His Kingdom. When dealing with new believers, we must treat them with respect, guidance, and inform them about things they may be doing that are wrong, without jumping to conclusions. Instead of assuming things or bullying them into positions...handle things with maturity. Take people aside and instruct in matters, rather than disgracing people publicly or reporting them here and there. Treat people the way you would like to be treated, showing where things are wrong, and why rather than expecting people to pick up on it through subtle behaviors and nasty attitudes.

Why people are so attracted to eastern, pagan, and non-Christian religions

If you watch television, research religion online, or take a survey crossing many different groups of people, you will note a distinct tone favoring eastern, pagan, and other non-Christian religious groups. There are many different theories as to why these groups are gaining popular ground, but I believe the basic reason lies in the matters we have discussed in this chapter. The general church focus on self and materialism is causing people to believe Christianity is about nothing more than worldly pursuits. A lack of apologetics, the basic inability for Christians to answer basic questions, the view that Christians are as worldly as everyone else is, and the general feeling that God is not the life focus of so many Christians has sent people wandering and searching for answers in other places. On the surface, eastern religion has the appearance of something deep. It sounds profound and enlightened because it is not easily understood without study. This draws people who desire to know something deeper than on a surface level. People who are looking for something and like the idea of having a gradual revelation come forth from it over time like the idea of these different religious systems.

I also believe the draw to such religions also attracts people who desire something that echoes social-consciousness. The Christian union with political conservatism has destroyed the objectivity of the church on secular matters and it has also clouded the church over from social-consciousness. There are people who genuinely believe issues such as sexual abuse or rape, inequalities between men and women, environmental issues, business corruption, and other social or systematic issues are ones that demand a spiritual perspective and answer. There are people who feel unwelcome in church because they feel their spirituality demands they step up and take stands on many issues the church finds uncomfortable or disconcerting. While you may know where the majority of churchgoers stand on issues such as homosexuality or abortion, you will seldom know where others stand on other issues, simply because they are never addressed.

We also see people who like the idea of practicing something with an individual sense of autonomy. Taught to find or observe certain things in the world without having to belong to a bigger group of people – a bigger group of critical, demanding, or dictating people – is appealing to many who have either been hurt by church or simply find the general guideline for religious assembly to be tiresome or difficult. There are those who do so out of a genuine sense of rebellion as well, but there are many who are simply searching for an answer and like the idea that they do not have to conform to a singular set of rules or principles.

Then there is the issue that people who do not fall into the general guidelines of church comforts often find themselves unwelcome or uncomfortable at church. As a childless woman, I know how uncomfortable it can be when people bring up such issues and feel the right to ask questions that have nothing to do with faith or spiritual matters. Too often people who are single, divorced, single parents, or somehow different do not feel comfortable in churches that endlessly promote family programs, "family values," and are in a rush to pair everyone off. We do not accept diversity in today's church because we fear that such will question conformity. People can still be within God's order and desire God's word if they are single, single parents, divorced, or otherwise different – and it is time the church stopped excluding such because it makes others question their own lives and choices.

Holiness does not mean we are all the same, it means we are set apart. Within the principle of holiness, this means each one of us is set apart by God and then joined to His other set apart people. We are each unique and each called by the Father into His will. People are leaving church and seeking out other options because they believe they are free to be more of themselves and pursue their own interests in a different atmosphere. If we want to bring them back – and bring in new individuals to church – we need to keep holiness in its proper context. Hammering beliefs over people's heads is not the way to do it...but showing love and integrity truly is.

CHAPTER EIGHT

IS RELIGION THE PROBLEM?

God, save us from people who mean well.
— Vikram Seth[1]

If you make your assessment according to the modern church, religion is the problem with the entire world. Religion is the reason we have wars, it is the reason people don't get along, it is the reason people are in bondage, and it is the reason people feel bad about themselves. Religion is blamed for everything, from why people don't know God to the reason why men don't put the toilet seat down after using the bathroom and women get PMS.

Have we stopped to ever consider if this general branding of religion as the world's greatest evil is fair? Sure, religion can have its issues, but every single one of our ancestors considered themselves to be religious people. Religion and religious devotion are found in every single country on the planet, which must give some merit to its existence. But what exactly is the purpose of religion? How does this purpose relate to salvation – and how can we use it to benefit our own evangelistic efforts? And, if this is all true – why are we so negative against religion in Christian circles today?

Do the unsaved know God?

Many people errantly assume that because non-Christians are branded as "non-believers," they know nothing about God. Too often, Christians make the mistake of treating non-Christians as if they are total idiots who are functioning on a level of "see God, see God run." Insulting people with this kind of condescending attitude doesn't help them see God, it just shows that Christians are as ignorant as non-believers think they are. It's a myth that the unsaved have never had a single experience with God, do not understand anything about God, and yes, that they have no knowledge of Him. The level of knowledge is, most likely different; they may not understand God in a proper way, nor in a saving way; but we, as Christians, need to establish what it means to have a knowledge of God so we can better know how to reach out and evangelize the world.

For this understanding, we are going to look at Romans 1:18-32:

God's wrath is being revealed from heaven against all the ungodly behavior and the injustice of human beings who silence the truth with injustice. This is because what is known about God should be plain to them because God made it plain to them. Ever since the creation of the world, God's invisible qualities–God's eternal power and divine nature–have been clearly seen, because they are understood through the things God has made. So humans are without excuse. Although they knew God, they didn't honor God as God or thank him. Instead, their reasoning became pointless, and their foolish hearts were darkened. While they were claiming to be wise, they made fools of themselves. They exchanged the glory of the immortal God for images that look like mortal humans: birds, animals, and reptiles. So God abandoned them to their hearts' desires, which led to the moral corruption of degrading their own bodies with each other. They traded God's truth for a lie, and they worshipped and served the creation instead of the creator, who is blessed forever. Amen.

That's why God abandoned them to degrading lust. Their females traded natural sexual relations for unnatural sexual relations. Also, in the same way, the males traded natural sexual relations with females, and burned with lust for each other. Males performed shameful actions with males, and they were paid back with the penalty they deserved for their mistake in their own bodies. Since they didn't think it was worthwhile to acknowledge God, God abandoned them to a defective mind to do inappropriate things. So they were filled with all injustice, wicked behavior, greed, and evil behavior. They are full of jealousy, murder, fighting, deception, and malice. They are gossips, they slander people, and they hate God. They are rude and proud, and they brag. They invent ways to be evil, and they are disobedient to their parents. They are without understanding, disloyal, without affection, and without mercy. Though they know God's decision that those who persist in such practices deserve death, they not only keep doing these things but also approve others who practice them.

Romans 1 is often quoted in certain contexts. Those contexts are almost always out of context to the meaning and purpose of the text. The reason why Romans 1 is so often quoted out of context is simple: we don't take it in the context of Romans 2, which we will discuss in a moment. Romans 1 and Romans 2 are two parts of a whole view of humanity God desires us to have.

As the Apostle Paul was called to work with the Gentiles, his experiences and writings with the individuals in church who came from a Gentile background were quite different from those experiences leaders would have had dealing with those from a Jewish background. We can get the basic gist of the issues the ancient Hebrews and then in New Testament times, the Jewish people (who were the descendants of the Hebrews) faced. The extremes in upholding the law (either totally abandoning it in the pursuit to be like everyone else or trying to force people into rigid codes of understanding it), being surrounded by nations that did not believe as they did, abandoning God, and dealing with the consequences therein were all things that plagued the Hebrew people in endless cycles throughout Bible times. The early apostles knew the Jewish people had a knowledge of God through the law, and, therefore, taught and handled matters differently with them than with the Gentiles. The term "Gentiles" (from a word that means "nations") was often used by the Jews in a derogatory context to indicate non-Jews were less favored and less important in the eyes of God, in an offensive way. This is what made the work of the Apostle Paul, one who held a dual citizenship of sorts: born as a Jew but also a Roman citizen by birth, so extraordinary. He had a unique perspective into both worlds, and was given the divine insight to understand and see God's hand in the conversion of the Gentiles. He recognized that salvation was for all, both Jew and Gentile, and that the Gentiles were not as devoid of God as the Jews of that time might have thought.

Romans 1 is not a special-interest, general thought to certain groups in existence today. It doesn't exist to bash the non-believer or an individual with what some would classify as an "alternative lifestyle." Rather, it is a view of the pagan knowledge of God. The point of Romans 1 is to prove that even though the Gentiles did not have the law, they still had some knowledge and experience with God. The way this was accomplished is clear – it came through a knowledge and understanding of nature. Since God is creator, anyone who has encountered His creation has come into a place where they can see God's hand at work. As a result of the bounty and beauty of all God has created, people have encountered God. This is true regardless of whether or not they recognize God properly in their lives.

Ancient pagan religions tended to be polytheistic, believing in many different gods, goddesses, and spirits. While most groups adopted a form of henotheism (believing one's deity is the chief or most relevant of all gods, but not denying the existence or relevance of others), the ancient pagans developed their system by noting natural cycles. Instead of believing there was one God behind all of it, they believed it took many deities to make things happen. They had a god for every natural cause: rain, drought, fertility, lighting, thunder, war, storms, aggression, sex, and beyond.

The gods of the ancient worlds went by different names, but the system was parallel across many different cultures. The fact that the same systematic parallel is found in a diversity of ancient places lets us know that the ancients all came to the same conclusions about the world around them, just from watching natural cycles. These conclusions can be summarized:

- There is a spiritual realm.

- There is more to life than just human existence followed by death.

- Creation has an origin that is beyond this world; it did not and does not self-subsist.

- There are consequences for things that we do in this life, and those consequences may last beyond the immediate world we see.

- The agricultural process, from preparing the soil all the way through to harvest, is not just a physical process; it reflects something spiritual.

- The changing seasons reflect spiritual principles.

- Nature as a whole is pointing us to something deeper; not just spiritual principles, but a person or being to come that is spiritual.

As a result, the ancient pagans believed many things that were contained in their annual festivals, feasts, and events that pictured different beliefs about their deities:

- Born of a virgin

- Had twelve disciples

- Taught and gained many followers

- Turned water into wine

- Walked on water

- Raised from the dead

The pagan world knew and understood certain things from their connection to the natural world. They knew just from observing times and seasons that spiritual things existed and how important those spiritual things were. They also could tell – just from watching nature – that important miracles and testimonies were to follow an important being who was not just any ordinary human being.

When you consider the pagan world did not have the law (they had nothing to clue them in on the coming of the Messiah in their doctrine), the fact that they picked up on all these diverse spiritual beliefs and facts is quite incredible. It proves that God's plan for humanity was truly for all of humanity, and that He knew down the ages the best possible ways to reach out so all of humanity would realize something about Him. He laid the foundation that all people might recognize their need for Christ and recognize Who He was.

It all sounds great and wonderful, right? Even the pagan knew about God! Doesn't that mean all religion is the same and all paths lead to God? Is Romans 1 the ultimate contradiction that there is only "one way" to God?

No, it's not. Romans 1 does affirm that all religions worldwide do have certain base elements in common. All religion strives to figure out spiritual things, and all religion does encourage people toward certain charitable and ethical principles. But Romans 1 does not exist to undermine the authority of Christ and the importance of believing in Him and of following Him in one's life. As we can see, Romans 1 does not just affirm the reality that the pagan knew of God, it also shows where the pagan went wrong. Instead of seeing God in nature and pursuing God, it clarifies the pagan turned to idolatry, worshipping the creature (in animalism, spiritism, and nature worship) rather than the Creator. The result from that singular point of idolatry was spiritual chaos, whereby followers of different pagan systems began using the understanding they did have of nature and spiritual things to practice magic. Through magic, they sought to control the elements and manipulate the spiritual realm, unto the end of all sorts of behaviors that were both unnatural and immoral. What they knew led them into a place of complete misunderstanding on spiritual matters and a distance where even though they had a knowledge of God, they did not know Him.

Beware self-righteousness

It would delight many Christians if the Apostle Paul had stopped right there, but he didn't. The purpose of his writing wasn't to shame the pagan, but to bridge – and overcome – the Jew/Gentile gap that was so prevalent in the early church. The Jews looked down on the Gentiles, believing they didn't know anything about God and were just an immoral, disobedient people. Romans 2:1-16 teaches us something important about religion – all religion, Judaism included:

Therefore you have no excuse, everyone of you who passes judgment, for in that which you judge another, you condemn yourself; for you who judge practice the same things. And we know that the judgment of God rightly falls upon those who practice such things. But do you suppose this, O man, when you pass judgment on those who practice such things and do the same yourself, that you will escape the judgment of God? Or do you think lightly of the riches of His kindness and tolerance and patience, not knowing that the kindness of God leads you to repentance? But because of your stubbornness and unrepentant heart you are storing up wrath for yourself in the day of wrath and revelation of the righteous judgment of God, who WILL RENDER TO EACH PERSON ACCORDING TO HIS DEEDS: to those who by perseverance in doing good seek for glory and honor and immortality, eternal life; but to those who are selfishly ambitious and do not obey the truth, but obey unrighteousness, wrath and indignation. There will be tribulation and distress for every soul of man who does evil, of the Jew first and also of the Greek, but glory and honor and peace to everyone who does good, to the Jew first and also to the Greek. For there is no partiality with God.

For all who have sinned without the Law will also perish without the Law, and all who have sinned under the Law will be judged by the Law; for it is not the hearers of the Law who are just before God, but the doers of the Law will be justified. For when Gentiles who do not have the Law do instinctively the things of the Law, these, not having the Law, are a law to themselves, in that they show the work of the Law written in their hearts, their conscience bearing witness and their thoughts alternately accusing or else defending them, on the day when, according to my gospel, God will judge the secrets of men through Christ Jesus.

Whoa! The Apostle Paul points out that the Jews acted just like the pagans! They were eligible for the same judgment, even though they lived under the law, as the pagans were! We also learn there is no partiality with God. While the Jewish people were established that Christ might come into the world, there was no moral superiority among those who had the knowledge of God. They were still sinners and still subject to judgment. The only difference – those who had the law would be subject and judged according to it because they had knowledge of it.

Romans 2:17-29 goes on to say:

But if you bear the name "Jew" and rely upon the Law and boast in God, and know His will and approve the things that are essential, being instructed out of the Law, and are confident that you yourself are a guide to the blind, a light to those who are in darkness, a corrector of the foolish, a teacher of the immature, having in the Law the embodiment of knowledge and of the truth, you, therefore, who teach another, do you not teach yourself? You who preach that one shall not steal, do you steal? You who say that one should not commit adultery, do you commit adultery? You who abhor idols, do you rob temples? You who boast in the Law, through your breaking the Law, do you dishonor God? For "THE NAME OF GOD IS BLASPHEMED AMONG THE GENTILES BECAUSE OF YOU," just as it is written.

For indeed circumcision is of value if you practice the Law; but if you are a transgressor of the Law, your circumcision has become uncircumcision. So if the uncircumcised man keeps the requirements of the Law, will not his uncircumcision be regarded as circumcision? And he who is physically uncircumcised, if he keeps the Law, will he not judge you who though having the letter of the Law and circumcision are a transgressor of the Law? For he is not a Jew who is one outwardly, nor is circumcision that which is outward in the flesh. But he is a Jew who is one inwardly; and circumcision is that which is of the heart, by the Spirit, not by the letter; and his praise is not from men, but from God.

The bottom line of what the Apostle Paul was trying to teach us is that all religion is the law, and we are all condemned by the systems we have all devised. Even though the law was given by God, it was interpreted by men, and its application was subject to human revelation. Even though the written law was there, the way it was interpreted and applied was through human understanding – the same as the way God's presence in nature was understood by the pagans. The understanding we have of God does not exist for self-serving purposes. God clarifies to us here in Romans 2 that self-righteousness is just as bad as idolatry. We may not want to hear that, think about it, or deal with it, but it's the truth.

While all religions do have certain things in common, the basic difference between Christianity and everyone else is our command to love our neighbor – yes, even our non-Christian neighbor. The major differentiating factor between Christianity and everything else is the fact that we believe God loved humanity enough to reach out and send His Son to atone for our sins. While other religions encourage individuals to reach out to their various gods, only Christianity can claim a God Who proved His love unto the end of the ultimate sacrifice of Christ. The difference needs to be the result – the product – us.

For Christians today, this means we need to be careful

when it comes to our attitudes about others and their beliefs. We need to refrain from making assumptions about others and from judging others. Every person in the world has sinned before God, and none is without need of salvation. Yes, the world needs to know the truth about God – but Romans 1 and 2 needs to call us to attention about what we are doing and why we are doing it.

Getting your info right

One of the major complaints I receive from non-believers about believers is the way in which they approach others about religious understandings. Evangelical circles are wrought with so-called "experts" in religion who label this group as a cult and that group as a false religion, and tell us very, very little about their actual belief systems. In fact, many of those so-called "experts" do not present the information they provide in a factual way. Many of them do not give facts or water those facts down with Christian teaching in an effort to draw the individual reading or watching the information away from that group. In between all of the lines there is a constant, underlying message: This group is wrong, we are right, so stop wondering about this false group.

This is a bad message to send. We live in a diverse world and if we are going to be all things to all people, we need to know about the beliefs and teachings of different people. It is possible to wonder what a group believes and not want to convert to that group's doctrinal understandings. As people called to go into all the world, we need to take a genuine interest in others, and that includes their beliefs as well as anything else in their lives.

On the other hand, most groups don't always present the most accurate information about themselves, especially when trying to show themselves to the outside world. People want others to think the best about them possible, and it doesn't take much to pad history over and gloss over the aspects of a religious history or leadership that appear less than desirable. It's a well-known fact that groups such as Scientology, Mormons, Jehovah's Witnesses, Armstrongists, and even many assorted Christian biographers tend to show their groups or their historical leaders in a light that isn't always completely accurate.

If you are going to be witnessing to a diverse audience, it's best to learn about religion, and get the information about that group right. This may mean researching the religion from different viewpoints or from a secular religious viewpoint to get a more accurate scope of the history and beliefs.

It is also vitally important that, when it comes to religion, Christians do the following:

- **Show respect for differing beliefs** – I didn't say you had to agree with them. I didn't say you had to believe them. Behind that belief is a person who believes in that doctrinal point or issue and takes it as a serious truth. You need to have enough respect for that person to respect that this is where they are right now and this is what they believe.

- **Show respect for customs** – Once again, I didn't say you have to agree with them. You don't have to practice them. But if you are on someone else's territory, in someone else's house, or visiting someone else's religious house of worship, you're on their turf – not you on theirs. You need to respect whatever customs they observe and religious practices to which they adhere, whether you want to partake of them, or not.

- **Don't act like you know more about their religion than they do** – I have undergraduate, graduate, and doctorate degrees in religion. I have spent more than fifteen years studying, visiting, and encountering people of different religious groups. If we are to be realistic, I know more about most religious groups than many nominal adherents do. I can tell a Mormon or a Jehovah's Witness things about their histories that even they don't know. But I've been on the other side of the table. To this day, people make offhand comments to me, such as, "I won't hold it against you that you used to be Catholic." These sorts of comments are often made by people who don't know the first thing about the Catholic Church and are going by the bits and pieces of a belief system they have heard about in passing in specific contexts. You may very well not know as much as you think and it's better to refrain from using information as a weapon. You aren't learning about a religious group to cause offense, but to understand where people are coming from, their specific needs, and specific ways you can talk so they can relate.

- **Be interested in people when they want to talk about their beliefs** – It's amazing what you can learn by listening to someone, especially when people know you are not just viewing them as a potential believer, but truly as a human being. Beliefs are a part of what makes us who we are.

What is religion and what purpose does it serve?

The Bible speaks to us very profoundly about religion and its purpose. Religion was employed all throughout the Old Testament through the law. It was not an evil thing, nor a dirty word; it was the way by which God's people reached out to Him. Whenever those people faltered from that purpose, they faltered far from God. If we look in the New Testament, we learn why religion was so important to the ancestors: it had a purpose. Its purpose is not to be followed to the letter or to be imposing, but to make mankind aware of their need for a Savior. We learn from studying Romans 1 and 2 that everyone - all of mankind - had knowledge of God and that all were without excuse - even the Gentiles - despite the fact that they did not have the written law. Theologians have debated the meaning of this for years, only to come up with different viewpoints on what this means. I believe that, if we rightly divide Romans 1, we understand why the Gentiles were also without excuse: because they too had a knowledge of God, even though they did not understand it. They knew of God through their religion, in watching nature, the times and the seasons, in learning God's principles through seed-time and harvest and beyond, and even though they were not brought to the full letter of the law, they still had enough knowledge from their religious experience to recognize they could not save themselves. Instead of seeking a true Savior, the Gentile religions worshipped a host of gods (who, if are carefully inspected, we can see many of them were types of Christ), idolizing nature and the creation rather than the Creator.

Religion is a means by which people have attempted to reach out to an understanding of the divine in the best way they knew how, as they saw it, and as they understood it. It is mankind's attempt to express devotion, honor, and establish guidelines for people to be spiritual in this world. Romans 1 and 2 clarifies whether Jew or Gentile, all of humanity missed the mark with religion. The Jews wanted to be like their neighbors and didn't want to do what God asked of them, and the Gentiles wound up completely off the mark. We can see in New Testament times how out of control Judaism was in the first century as the leaders began to impose legislation upon people, passing such off as the Word of God. They loved their religious customs and pageantries, the way they were treated by others, and how advanced everyone thought them to be. The Gentiles also reached such a point: it is still common in various religions around the world to sell girls as temple prostitutes and to worship religious leaders as gods on earth. What started out as a pointing to something else - and which can be and is an effective tool to make people recognize they can't save themselves - became about self-worship and self-idolatry through those various means.

What we can see from all of this is that when people start to go beyond the bounds, religion's purpose is lost, until it becomes something else, something sinister, something that enslaves people. Being 'religious' can lead someone to the Savior as they learn all the rules, regulations, and sign points won't get you there. God knew that. Now if we could only know that, and recognize religion is a part of God's plan. It is not the end of it, but it leads one to where they need to get to be to recognize the Lord on it.

Religion makes us aware that we need a Savior. It lets all of us know that there is something bigger than each and every one of us and we need to explore deeper to find what that is. In religion, we start looking for Christ. We will not find Him if we keep trying to look there – but we will learn that we truly need Him.

If religion isn't the problem, what is?

Many modern Christians are surprised to learn the word "religion" is actually found in the Bible, and the context in which it is used is never negative (Acts 25:19, Acts 26:5, Colossians 2:23, James 1:26-27). It is used to refer to belief systems, in an objective sense. The only distinction made between religion in the Bible that some religion is true, some is man-made, and some is false. For example: James 1:26-27 reads:

If anyone thinks himself to be religious, and yet does not bridle his tongue but deceives his own heart, this man's religion is worthless. Pure and undefiled religion in the sight of our God and Father is this: to visit orphans and widows in their distress, and to keep oneself unstained by the world.

The clear usage of the word "religion" here is not as some sort of "religious spirit" that is spoken of as needing to be cast out. It is speaking of one's belief system, and how that belief system is proven useful or worthless by the way people conduct themselves.

This proves we are using the word "religious" in an incorrect context today and that incorrect context is causing us to create an enemy in religion that does not really exist. The Bible does clarify the problem is not religion in and of itself, and it also tells us the very thing that is a problem; and that is legalism.

Legalism is a belief in upholding rigid code of understanding. In legalism, one is penalized and judged by an interpretation of one's doctrinal understanding, the Bible, or other code, without any consideration for understanding or love. We could describe it as a partial flexibility: legalists decide who and what will receive mercy, who and what will receive the benefit of the doubt, and hold some to the rules while excusing others. Legalism decides who will be judged, who will not be judged, and how the penalty will come across, in every situation.

Legalism never considers self-examination, and it leaves no room for mercy. It enforces rules and regulations at whim, and makes people believe that they will never, ever be good enough or able to reach out to God in a way that will be satisfactory to Him. You can work a system forever, perform its tasks, do them daily, show up, and try, try again, but the system will, in the end, turn on you, too. It is the opposite of grace, which recognizes that while we cannot do it on our own, God reaches out to us and we are able to experience His unmerited favor in return.

It's ironic that most of the biggest noisemakers against religion tend to be some of the most legalistic, unforgiving people you will ever meet. Christians can be as "unreligious" as they want to be, but still be legalistic. If the system is imposed, time and time again, without exception – unless, of course, it is someone that we seek to make an exception for – the system is legalistic.

Legalism keeps people from God because it distorts the very nature of God as unjust, uncaring, and unloving. Our God distorted by legalism does not appear to care about humanity. It gives God the appearance of a taskmaster who cares nothing about those engaging in tasks. Just as paganism distorts the image of God, legalism distorts His nature. It gives people the power to speak on behalf of God through rules and regulations that He never intended, nor created.

Legalism keeps people away from God, period. It is a bad thing that causes people to believe false things about Him and adhere to false systems. It has a root spirit which needs to be dealt with and addressed, but legalism is not specifically a religious problem. Yes, legalism can take on the form of religion and exercise its punitive beliefs through a system, but legalism can take on any form (even atheists can be legalistic). It can manifest in a work environment, family life, society, and any semblance of thinking. Doing away with religion doesn't eradicate legalism – doing away with legalism does. We need to stop the war on religion, trying to eradicate something we can build upon – and get rid of the legalistic demon that seeks power and control at every turn.

Why we want to get away from religion today

I believe the confusion between legalism and religion has a much more sinister root, one of pride and arrogance. Before each and every one of us living right now were ever born, there were people who lived, had faith, and experienced God in ways they could understand based on the best knowledge they had of Him at the time. Maybe some of what they did was a little extreme, maybe some of it seemed a little out-of-balance or austere to us today, but they were believers, doing the best they knew how, with what they had. They were figuring this "faith thing" out, much like we are today, with less to go on than we have now. Many of them were illiterate, many did not have the opportunity to go to school or learn, and along with learning came sacrifices most don't even entertain today, such as celibacy or monastic life. Many of them reached a point where they could not interact in a "normal" way with others, because their desire for truth, life, and purity because so intense. Despite the peripherals, they were people who sought God intensely, loved Him with all they had, and wanted to experience the wholeness of God, receiving all He had for them.

Becoming a "people without religion" divorces us from the many efforts, steps, and works our ancestors took to be people of faith. It holds us above them, looks down upon them, and treats people of generations past as if they were "unsaved" people. This is based in a belief that people today have some sort of greater insight or revelation than those of past generations, when we really don't. Despite many archaeological finds, scholarly studies into language and scriptural history, a myriad of Bible translations, and the extensive system of higher education available in today's world, the overall Christian population is still quite Biblically illiterate, theologically illiterate, and void of spiritual understanding. In faith, many of us aren't any better than our ancestors used to be – but unlike those who were that way because there was no other way, many of us are that way by choice. We choose not to educate ourselves out of fear that learning about things might change our viewpoints, attitudes, or regard for others in this world. The best way to do this is to divorce ourselves from our ancestors, because then we can feel better about them and substitute general spiritual enlightenment for judgment.

Christian history is a must for every Christian. It is a must because it gives us a sense of the long road trod prior to our existence and, in many circles, prior to the founding of our immediate churches and ministries. Several somebodies throughout history lived, died, suffered unspeakable persecution, and fought for their beliefs, whether in whole or in part. If we, as Christians, divorce ourselves from our powerful history, we will lose sight of the truth about our faith and even the very fabric of our own evangelism: once upon a time, every one of us that claims to be a believer once was not. Someone, somewhere in time went before us and helped show us the way, as well. Perfect or imperfect, whole or in part, they stood for something that someone in another age stood for, and so on, and so forth. When we have history, we realize it doesn't matter what we call our system. It doesn't matter if we call it spirituality, a relationship with God, or yes, even religion – it simply matters that we have it, and it exists.

Evangelism among believers and doctrinal debates

The word on the street is that evangelism among professing Christians – where one Christian of one denomination is evangelizing a Christian of another denomination – is on the rise. In fact, from the rumors I have heard, the majority of "conversions" are from one denomination to another. Realizing this needs to call us to attention for a few reasons. The first is that the church is not genuinely heeding its call to evangelism. The purpose of evangelism is to bring people to the faith who don't know about the Lord or who are far from Him. Having someone join your church who belonged to another church doesn't really count as evangelism. What this is more properly asserted as is doctrinal conversion, whereby one changes something in their doctrine, while their foundational belief remains the same. The second reason why we need to pay attention to this is because efforts toward evangelism are being spent more on other people who already know the Lord because of variances in belief than on the unbeliever. This means there is more conflict among Christians of different backgrounds because everyone is seen as a potential convert – no one is safe.

The resulting conflict means in a world where everyone has an opinion, people "convert" via doctrinal debate. It's the hope that "my doctrine is going to be so convincing, your doctrine won't be able to stand up in light of it." While I won't say that it never works, I think the rate of conversion from it is probably quite low. As Christians, we should be putting our efforts into reaching the lost, not looking for opportunities to argue with other believers. While I agree that yes, sometimes what we believe needs to be corrected, we are fooling ourselves if we think that such is accomplished through endless argumentation and debate.

The following is from my book, *About My Father's Business: Professional Ministry For Kingdom Leaders* on the topic of debate:

"The ministry of apologetics used to be the standard means for the defense of the faith. Biblical scholars spent hours comparing texts, original languages, history, context, traditions, and various methods of interpretation to form a solid approach to Biblical understanding. The art of apologetics, which provided concrete proof for belief beyond a verse here and there, has all but died and been replaced with intense emotionalism and politics. Stepping back and learning about matters helps us to form a more polished approach to our defense and reminds us that we are defending the faith, rather than our emotions. While faith certainly stirs the emotions, neither faith nor ministry, are to be things that operate on emotions. If we are employing emotions in our debates, then we are operating an essential aspect of our ministry via emotions. This must end here and now because it creates a negative witness.

"The Bible advises us to avoid needless debates (2 Timothy 2:23, Titus 3:9). This means there is more than one type of debate. A debate can be productive – a learning experience, one that facilitates discussion and interest – or it can be needless. A needless debate is any argumentation that has no purpose to go anywhere. Some people just want to fight or have people think they are right. Sometimes debates get out of hand because they are designed to do so. Some people just don't have the ability to handle a debate-type situation. Sometimes the debate just isn't worth our time. This is where discernment comes in, in a powerful way.

"A productive debate seeks to respectfully discuss matters and present viewpoints. It looks at different angles of an issue and examines those issues from research or evidence. Debate is not emotion-based, but presents a reasoned viewpoint of a critique or argument. In productive debate, there is no interruption and everyone is given the opportunity to present the appropriate viewpoint. Productive debate can be very effective in witnessing the Gospel as topics arise and the Word can be used therein to be shown to apply to whatever the topic at hand may be. Remain poised and eloquent, not shouting, name-calling, or interrupting. Present a reasoned argument.

"A needless debate has no purpose except to argue with others. Typically it is a random, nonsensical topic that doesn't have any significance and has no power to change anyone's life. In other words, it is a topic that doesn't really have an answer, just random opinions. The purpose is to go back and forth, back and forth, interrupt, create disorder and confusion, and outlet anger. Most of the time, the debate causes a level of frustration that causes a fever-pitch to get someone so out of control, it 'seems' to prove the other side's point. Discernment calls us to step away from such debates that are mere traps to discredit the work of the Kingdom.

"A discussion is a conversation between two or more people. It is like debate with the exception that discussion is more open, more intimate, than just debating a topic. It is about conversing, sharing, and building. Akin to discussion is dialogue. Dialogue is an "open door" of communication. It is more than a mere conversation: it is a continuing discussion on a matter. In the Kingdom, we need to be prepared to answer questions as the start to dialogue. When people come to us with a question, it is often in search of something beyond an answer. Sometimes people do just want an answer to a question, but much of the time they are looking to talk about something bigger than the mere question. In dialogue, we must listen and truly speak as directed to bring about the necessary revelation within a dialogue.

"We also must pay attention to the areas of disagreement in ministry. It is inevitable that we will encounter a minister, ministry, individual, or issue that we will disagree with. How much we agree with someone is not nearly as relevant as how we handle our disagreements. There are a few keys to handling disagreements below, as found below:

- **Is this an essential or non-essential disagreement?** – Ego is a big factor in life. We can try and pretend it isn't, but it is. That having been said, it is amazing the things people magnify because of a bruised ego. Not everyone in the entire world is going to agree with us about every little thing in life. If we are waiting for this to happen, we will have a long and lonely wait. There are some things we cannot unite ourselves unto because they are in contradiction to Kingdom principle. We can't unite with leaders who are out of God's will for leadership, we can't participate in events that mix truth and error, we can't allow ourselves to be abused or mistreated, and we likewise can't expose ourselves to harm by mingling ourselves with error. That having been said, we can put aside personal opinions or differences outside of the realm of truth and work with God's people in the building of His Kingdom. Working with differences of this nature helps us to grow as people and grow in our own viewpoints, recognizing we aren't the only people in the world working in the Kingdom of God.

- **How should I handle this matter?** – Sometimes we need to speak up, and sometimes we need to shut up. Sometimes we need to voice issues and sometimes we need to let them rest. Disagreements can be handled in more than one way. Recognizing this – and stepping back to examine a situation so it can be handled rightly – can make a huge difference in the outcome of a disagreement.

- **What is behind the disagreement?** – Disagreements aren't always about the subject matters that appear on the surface. Sometimes there are deep issues behind disagreements between people that either need to resolve or they need to part ways. If there's something that keeps coming up in every situation that manifests behind the things that manifest, it may be time to do some examination about the situation and people with whom you find yourself involved.

- **Watch tone, language, and control** – Disagreements get out of hand because people get out of hand in an attempt to try and get another person to agree with or see their viewpoint. It doesn't take much for a situation to get totally out of control because of such an emotional rush and high. We can't control other people in disagreement, but we can control ourselves. Watch tone, sarcasm, language, and personal disciplines in disagreement. If a situation is getting too hot to handle, walk away from it, stop talking, leave, or do whatever else is necessary to handle your own level of control. If someone else wants to be disgraceful, leave them to do it alone.

- **Keep order and respect in mind** – Remember the establishment of order we spoke of in an earlier chapter and remember to maintain a specific balance of order when dealing with elders and those who have authority over you. It's also a good practice to maintain respect with anyone in the Body of believers. Just because you don't like what someone has to say does not give you the right to become unruly and behave without self-control. How we carry ourselves in areas of debate, disagreement, dialogue, and discussion is not about anybody but us. We can walk away from a situation with total dignity if we keep ourselves controlled and well-behaved."

Understanding stereotypes

The last thing we need to examine in the area of religion is the issue of stereotyping. Even though Christians jump up and down and want to avoid the "religion" label, as far as the world is concerned, Christianity is just another religion. We talked a little bit earlier about the difference between Christianity and other religions, and I am going to reiterate here – the difference people need to see is in us.

People judge the whole of a thing by a part of it. Is this unfair? Of course it is. We have talked extensively about why this is wrong on many issues in our society, but it doesn't change the fact that people make their judgments based on the first or few impressions they have of a singular person. There is a reason why groups that heavily engage in evangelistic promotions put so much emphasis on appearance and timing – because they know they only have a few minutes to make a first impression.

That means people today are coming along with whatever pre-conceived ideas they already have about Christianity and are already judging the whole of the faith by one person, rather than assess the one individual person by the whole of belief and expectation. It's no secret many public figures have done serious damage to the appearance of Christianity, and the world is watching carefully, thinking this is how all Christians act, think, and behave.

How you talk to someone else – how you approach someone else – how you interact with someone else – who is of a differing belief system – is very, very relevant. It must be done with honesty and respect. You have the opportunity to not only change someone's stereotyped image of a Christian, you also have the opportunity to change someone's life. Use the opportunity wisely.

Chapter Nine

Church Hurt

A brother offended is harder to be won than a strong city,
And contentions are like the bars of a citadel.
– Proverbs 18:19

When I first set to write this book, this chapter was not included. It came up later as I realized how prevalent what we've come to brand as "church hurt" is and how important it is to address it.

Those of us who have been in church for more than a few years have all heard the term, *"There's no hurt like a church hurt."* When people get hurt by someone and associate it with the church, it sets off a whole process, which we will discuss here. Yes, we have all heard of church hurt, but have we ever stopped to think about why the church has an entire designation of hurt unique to it? There is no such thing as "mosque hurt," "ashram hurt," "temple hurt," "cult hurt," or "guru hurt," even though we all know there are people who have been hurt or abused by these systems, so what is it about hurt in the church that has caused us to have our own genre of hurt? What do we, as a church, need to look at in order to fix this string of "hurt" that we seem to perpetuate – and how is "church hurt" relevant to the work of evangelism?

What is church hurt?

Church hurt is a general term used to describe a sense of pain, offense, or hurt one encountered from someone who was either part of a church group or claims to be a part of a group. The perpetrator of the hurt can be a member, a leader, or someone who claims to be involved, but isn't as involved as they claim. The person who encounters the hurt may be a nominal member, a new member, a long-time member, a fringe member who isn't very involved, or even someone in leadership. Sometimes those who have experienced church hurt have taken offense to something minor, while others who have experienced it have truly been deeply hurt by something abusive or offensive that happened to them.

The individual who encounters church hurt usually cites the experience or experiences as the reason they are either hesitant to belong to a Christian group again or why they have given up on God, church, or spiritual things in general. For this reason, we, as a church, must take church hurt very seriously and examine where, why, and how such has occurred.

An offensive church

The church today is a contrast in unbalanced extremes. There are those who are extremely offensive, and those who are easily offended. As a result, we hear a lot of teaching against the "spirit of offense," without considering the proper order that should occur when someone either is offensive or is offended. The thing I want us to look at, however, is the fact that offense is such a notable facet within today's church. The reason church hurt is so common is because people are both offensive and easily offended. With a church high on emotionalism, battles for control and political dominance, and a general sense of people not knowing their place and operating without humility, church hurt is the result. A church of extremes breeds offenders and offense.

That means we need to step back and take a big, deep breath before we talk and we need to carefully examine and judge our own motives. Alas, I am not saying something new.

For decades, true church leaders have been advising members to behave rightly and speak rightly. Still, people aren't listening.

There is more than one context to offense. Sometimes people cause trouble and are always getting their feelings hurt, because they use offense as an excuse not to do what they should be doing. Such are forever getting their feelings hurt for one reason or another and use such to justify not stepping out, not going deeper in faith, and not making commitments. Offense is, for such a weapon and nobody and nothing will overcome it without deliverance.

That having been said, I think we need to be careful not to write off all people who have experienced church hurt as overly sensitive, easily offended people. As one who has encountered church hurt, I can testify that it did offend me and it did put me in a place where I got away from being right with God in my life. It wasn't that I was overly sensitive or trying to get out of something, but that I encountered something that really did cause me hurt in my life and that hurt led me astray. There are people who are genuinely hurt by others in the church in a way that they are grieved beyond words and no longer know how to interact with other believers spiritually. The truth is that Christians in general have a reputation for being vile and offensive in their opinions. While it's fine to have an opinion, a conviction, a belief system, and so on and so forth, it's not fine to shove whatever it is you think down other people's throats. Christians are very, very guilty of this behavior; of imposing their own thoughts on everyone else, all the while expecting everyone else to line up accordingly.

Sometimes being a Christian means keeping your mouth shut. You do not have to advocate for everything so vocally and with such virulence. The entire world does not have to agree with you for you to have your opinion. Still, we live in a world where people do what I just mentioned without thinking twice about it, which means church hurt can and will happen.

It is also not a big secret that abuse is prevalent in many professing Christian circles. Whether cults, groups that break away from their original denominations, or non-denominational churches, stories of leaders who sexually assault or molest their members, tales of child abuse, or other horror stories, such incidents always make the evening news. More positive images of church life and Christian witness never hit the papers. This can lead people to believe all churches are like the ones where they experienced abuse and believe all Christians are the same.

We've forgotten that actions speak louder than words. It's great to tell people you "love them with the love of the Lord," but it's a lot better if you show them. When people have been genuinely hurt, offended, or abused, they need to experience a love that transforms, not an attitude that holds them at bay or brushes them off with cute, trite sayings.

Why church hurt hurts

Church hurt hurts because it is something that we believe is not supposed to exist. If God is love and His people are supposed to be about love, church hurt has a special sting because it is wrong on many levels. It violates the love we are to have for one another in the Body, it violates the place and positioning God has given us in the Body, and it violates our sense of spirituality. In many people, this causes an upheaval in one's spiritual perspectives: it can affect how they see God, how they see their relationship with Him, and how they view the church as a whole. Church hurt causes emotional blockage to discernment where everyone and everything starts to look the same.

People associate the whole with the part, as we discussed in the last chapter. People can associate church hurt on all sorts of levels: the reason why they had family problems growing up, the reason they have difficulties or issues as an adult, the reason things happened the way they did, or the reason why they have issues with God. Church hurt is a long-standing hurt; it is often complicated within people's minds and many things (whether related or not) become closely associated with it.

Church hurt and evangelism

Many people you will encounter in evangelism have some form of church hurt in their lives. The way church hurt may manifest itself is often different in each person. Some are very bitter, some are notably wounded, others may be angry and hostile to church in general. Some will want to discuss their story or talk about what they encountered and others won't be so apt to discuss what they experienced. Also, do not be surprised to see people in different places as a result of church hurt. The same kind of experience can cause different people to react in different ways. Some may be genuinely looking to get back into church and back into a restoration with God, but just don't know where to go with it. Others might want nothing whatsoever to do with Christianity or God.

The answer to church hurt is the healing power and love of Christ. How it comes forth to such individuals may vary. The most important step to evangelizing someone who has encountered church hurt is to be there for them. Be more than just someone looking to convert them, but someone who is genuine and sincere about representing God's love and transforming power to them.

We should be able to identify with those who have experienced church hurt because every single one of us who has been in church has been hurt by someone else in church at some point in time. Even though the experiences we've had might not have driven us away from God or from church, we can empathize with the feelings of hurt, offense, and mistreatment that we have all encountered.

What helped you to move past the hurts and offenses that you have encountered in church throughout the years? Was it someone who kept on you about it and acted like a nag, someone else who condemned you and tried to be in control of the situation, or was it genuinely someone who took the time to listen, care, and be there for you? In addition to taking some time and sorting some of it out, having supportive, caring people around makes all the difference in the life of a hurt person.

People who have experienced church hurt often don't need as much doctrinal education, but they need a true healing touch and a true reorientation of the faith and the love of the Father. With someone who has experienced church hurt, the goal of evangelism is to bring them to a place where they are able to experience such. Hurt people need to know that love exists despite the hurt and that healing is a real facet, a real thing. This means evangelism with a person who has been hurt is a point-of-contact; it is an open door, a persistent love, rather than a doctrinal argument or nasty anger about the fact that they have left church. In such a situation, you need to be the church and show forth that God's love can transcend each and every hurt.

CHAPTER TEN

PRODIGALS AND THOSE WHO LOVE THEM

*Every parent is at some time the father of the unreturned prodigal, with
nothing to do but keep his house open to hope.*
– John Ciardi[1]

My sister, Natalie (name has been changed) was a child and teen who rebelled against everything and nothing for no good reason. My mom had a way of keeping us in line without being overly strict about it. She was also, as a rule, a very fair parent. This didn't matter to my sister. She still had to get her point across, no matter how ridiculous it might have been. When secretly dying Easter eggs in the kitchen one year, she dropped dye all over the new linoleum floor. Her answer was to cover it with a towel. When asked why she was standing on a towel, her answer was, "What towel?" She did the whole Goth/dress in black thing when it was still considered "punk." She came down the stairs one morning, having dyed her hair black in the shower. She pierced her own ears multiple times, having somewhere between five and six piercings in one ear. So, my mother would say, "Is that a new hole in your ear?" to which my sister would say, "No, it's been there all along, you just never noticed it before." Apparently my sister didn't consider that my mother would catch on, as her memory was (and is) quite good, and she would realize Natalie was not born with six holes in one ear. She told lies - all the time - big lies, not little or moderate ones. One of her lies ran the risk of putting someone in jail, without cause. She invited trouble, announced she was emancipating herself at sixteen and then moved out, and spent several years of her life in problematic situations. She was pregnant and living with a drug dealer who reportedly grew marijuana in his closets and had a dog who tore up baby clothes. She was one who came forth, time and time again, with horror stories, dramatic events, and complicated encounters. Once she moved away from where we lived in New York, she would come back to visit from time to time. It was always something new - new self-destructive behaviors, destructive jobs that put her at risk (and one of which made her permanently ill), destructive relationships, and constantly destructive choices. With her, nothing was ever simple.

I remember watching my mom with my sister. She is eight years older than I am, and she is the only sister I remember watching grow up in any semblance at all, as my other three sisters are more than eleven years older than I am, and two of them were in their twenties, grown, and out of the house before I was even born. When I was little, she was my favorite sister. She was fun and funny, and that rebellious streak gave her a quirky quality that was entertaining to a little kid. As I started to get older, I got tired of her. The quirkiness became embarrassing and her self-destructive tendencies made it impossible to ever relate to her on any kind of level. She was dominating and controlling, and had an incessant need for attention. I used to wonder where it came from, as she certainly wasn't a neglected child. Sure, my father was abusive, but he was to all of us, and he made a special effort with her and one of my other sisters that he didn't make with the rest of us. Time after time after time, Natalie had issues. Time after time after time, my mother interceded, prayed, helped, reached out, and advocated for her healing...until one day, my sister just didn't come back...and my mother had to let her go.

I learned years after the fact that right before my sister's departure, she spoke of visions and signs she was seeing in the spiritual realm. My mother urged her to come to where she needed to be, but she refused. I never thought about it at the time, but in hindsight, it must have been such a difficult thing to watch the gifts of God go undeveloped. She was not a stupid person, by any means; at one point, she talked about being a lawyer. Watching my sister walk away not just from her and the family, but from God as well, must have been something difficult to see, beyond words.

My sister is my mother's "prodigal."

Just tonight I heard another mother's words, her heart, her pain over the choices her prodigal children made and are making. It took me back to my mom and the experience she had with my sister. Then the Lord took me to the Word within my mind and the story of the "prodigal son." We've all heard about the story of the "prodigal son." To many of us it's a nice story that makes us feel all warm and fuzzy, blah, blah, blah. We think about the story in judgment of the son and his unwise choices. We look down on him. We don't consider the story in its context or the purpose in that story. We don't think about the father. We don't think about ourselves.

The father and the son

"There was a man who had two sons. The younger one said to his father, 'Father, give me my share of the estate.' So he divided his property between them. Not long after that, the younger son got together all he had, set off for a distant country and there squandered his wealth in wild living. (Luke 15:11-13, NIV)

The man in this story was asked by his prodigal for his share in his father's estate. There's a facet of this we don't ever consider. This man worked all his life. The estate was his work, his legacy, his portion. He worked hard to give his best for his children, like so many parents. He wanted them to have everything they could, and to want for nothing. He didn't work for himself, and he certainly didn't work to watch his investment fall by the wayside into squandered living. Yet, he gave his prodigal his share of the estate.

We all know that the father knew the son was going to squander it. His plan was to get off that farm and go experience the "good life." He was going to drink. He was going to carouse. He was going to have the best clothes, the best shoes, the best of everything. He would eat and have more than his fill. This life, this labor, this farm work his father did was beneath the prodigal. These were his aspirations in life that we know he brought up every time something happened that was less than what he wanted for himself. This pursuit was a carefully executed plan in the works for long before he ever left home.

Even though I have no natural children, I have dealt with the rebellious spiritual child and know how difficult it is to watch someone create a plan totally against what God has for them and then have to step back, allowing them all they need to walk in that plan. The father in this story is the definition of "tough love." Sure, he knew such a life was not what his son needed, but he also knew his son had to figure that out for himself. Parents today talk too much. They try to reason with their children and persuade them to see things from their perspective. The heart is right - it is to avoid their children heartache and pain. What they don't realize is some things need to be learned the hard way, through heartache and pain. Both natural and spiritual parents need to recognize a prodigal when they have one and step back, allowing God to teach them through consequence. It doesn't make it any easier to know they will gain an invaluable spiritual education from the hard road they take. However, when in these situations, the answer is to give what is allowed according to precept and allow them to go their own way.

Let them go their own way

After he had spent everything, there was a severe famine in that whole country, and he began to be in need. So he went and hired himself out to a citizen of that country, who sent him to his fields to feed pigs. He longed to fill his stomach with the pods that the pigs were eating, but no one gave him anything. (Luke 15:14-16, NIV)

We can gather that a great number of years passed in this story. The prodigal didn't leave home, spend all his money in a week, and the famine start the week after that. There is a long pause of time in here where we can note something important: The father did not chase after his son. He didn't constantly try to find him to send him a birthday card, make sure he was well-cared for, or that he had enough money. In other words he did not enable him. The son had his goal in mind and his father left him to do that. I know, without a doubt, that the father thought about the son. I am sure he had times when he wondered where he was, what he was doing, what was going on in his life. The temptation was there to chase after his son…but he resisted that temptation because the son would never learn if he knew dad was trying to intervene. He had to let go of his son and let God work out whatever needed working out. This doesn't mean he stopped caring, it means he accepted his limitations and didn't try to do for his son what his son had to do for himself.

"To let go does not mean to stop caring, it means I can't do it for someone else."[2]

The going was great until the prodigal ran out of money, and then there was a famine in the country. He wasn't prepared for a lean time, or a time when things would be out of his plan. Same is true with all prodigals - they have their goals and ideals, but they don't have their preparations. Well, desperate times call for desperate measures: the prodigal winds up at what twelve-step programs call "rock bottom." When someone hits "rock bottom," they cannot fall any farther down. There is nowhere left for them to go, except to admit they've reached a point where they need help. In the prodigal's rock bottom, he had to hire himself out as a laborer, doing the work I am sure he felt once was beneath him. He was sent to tend to the unclean, that which, according to Jewish custom, was not even considered fit for eating. Even in that mode, he still didn't find what he needed.

The prodigal had to address his situation. That is the end result of rock bottom. Before someone reaches this point, they don't feel they have to make a decision about their situation. They carry on in a state of denial, thinking things aren't where they may really be and talk themselves into believing they are in actuality all right. The point of rock bottom is different for all prodigals. For some, they hit the thud of a pebble while others have to hit a boulder over and over and over again. The point isn't what brings the individual to rock bottom...it's that, through that experience, they finally reach the point where it's time to do the right thing. Prodigals, dealing in rebellion, can walk as very selfish people. They don't do the right thing readily and have a hard time seeing to do the right thing in a situation, even if the situation is hurting them. Rock bottom makes them see the truth about themselves and others, and yes...even those who love them.

A place of humility

When he came to his senses, he said, 'How many of my father's hired men have food to spare, and here I am starving to death! I will set out and go back to my father and say to him: Father, I have sinned against heaven and against you. I am no longer worthy to be called your son; make me like one of your hired men.' So he got up and went to his father. (Luke 15:17-20, NIV)

The son had to humble himself...something very difficult for him to do. He had his plan, and had to face that his plan didn't work. In the eyes of the culture of his day and even by our standards today, he wasn't worthy of his father's love. He wasn't worthy of being called his son, and having squandered the inheritance, he was no longer a part of the promise (think Esau and Jacob). Setting back after so many years would cause him to lose face and also risk great rejection from his father.

"But while he was still a long way off, his father saw him and was filled with compassion for him; he ran to his son, threw his arms around him and kissed him. "The son said to him, 'Father, I have sinned against heaven and against you. I am no longer worthy to be called your son.' "But the father said to his servants, 'Quick! Bring the best robe and put it on him.

Put a ring on his finger and sandals on his feet. Bring the fattened calf and kill it. Let's have a feast and celebrate. For this son of mine was dead and is alive again; he was lost and is found.' So they began to celebrate. (Luke 15:20-24, NIV)

The father's hurt, anguish, and pain comes down to this moment when he realizes his prodigal has returned. The pain he went through all those years was a type of the anguish and distress God experiences when He has to let any of His prodigals go their own way and discover for themselves where their own ways will lead them. That hurting mother or father, spiritual mother or father, grandmother, relative, or other person in the prodigal's life comes to a deep and profound understanding of God's love and His mercy toward all of us. He provides the best for us through creation and through salvation in His Son, Jesus Christ, the perfect offering for sin. Watching people walk away from God's most perfect gift doesn't bring God joy and pleasure, it grieves Him in a way none of us can describe. Watching people walk to Him brings forth a joy and gladness we can't easily understand, either. The return of a prodigal of any sort is a joy and blessing beyond measure to the heart of God.

The "other son"

"Meanwhile, the older son was in the field. When he came near the house, he heard music and dancing. So he called one of the servants and asked him what was going on. 'Your brother has come,' he replied, 'and your father has killed the fattened calf because he has him back safe and sound.'" The older brother became angry and refused to go in. So his father went out and pleaded with him. But he answered his father, 'Look! All these years I've been slaving for you and never disobeyed your orders. Yet you never gave me even a young goat so I could celebrate with my friends. But when this son of yours who has squandered your property with prostitutes comes home, you kill the fattened calf for him!' "'My son,' the father said, 'you are always with me, and

everything I have is yours. But we had to celebrate and be glad, because this brother of yours was dead and is alive again; he was lost and is found.'" (Luke 15:25-32, NIV)

The majority of the church today could fall into the category of the "other son." We don't talk a lot about him. In some ways, he was probably very justified in how he felt. He spent years at his father's side, laboring in a way and paying a price to be the "good son." It must have felt like a slap in the face to have spent so many years as the responsible one. I think something else underlined this brother, however. I think he was jealous. He was jealous and envious because his brother got to do things and live in a way that he would have loved to live...but was too "upright" to do so. In his eyes, his brother got to go off, do everything he wanted, and then came back once he got into trouble...and was even rewarded for that. He was angry because his brother got the good life, and he got to work hard. He judged the worthiness of his brother to receive his father's love. Are we not like that now in the modern church? We spend so much time moralizing we fail to do people any good. People fall into sin. Things happen in people's lives that lead them down a path they should not always go. Over here in the church...too many of us hate them for the "good time" they get to have while we have to stay over here, all proper and upright without so much as a party! We point fingers, condemn and fail to help the prodigals. The prodigal didn't just have a father, he also had a brother - which means that now prodigals don't just have biological or spiritual parents, they also have brothers and sisters in Christ. Do we rejoice when God blesses them, or do we scoff and act angry because we don't get the portion we want?

We never know what God is doing in someone's life, or the way in which He will reach someone. This is why we must watch our judgments of others. We don't know what people went through to reach the point they've reached, and we may not see what an earthly, spiritual, or heavenly parent may see. We also forget that being a prodigal is about more than just running off and doing physical things that one may want to do. A prodigal can take any form. There are literal prodigals, as my sister was, and as are many children of parents I know.

There are spiritual prodigals, those who rebel and run from their call at any cost, out of disobedience, fear, or both. There are emotional prodigals, people who just want to escape and don't want to face the realities of life and the consequences of behavior. No matter the type of prodigal, finding their way back to our Father always rates the joy and celebration of finding them back where they belong - in the place of restoration.

Being the prodigal

We've all been someone's prodigal at some point, even if we are God's prodigal, and nobody else's. Some prodigals may never make it back; my sister is one such case. Some natural and spiritual parents always live with the pain and sorrow of having to make difficult choices and step up as parents, allowing God to work in ways that may not make sense to us in the flesh. Behind every returned prodigal is a loving parent who made the difficult decision to trust God with their children and trust Him for their life and peace in a deeper way than any of us can ever imagine. Lift that parent up, don't make the prodigal's parent the enemy. Often we pray for the prodigals, as we should. Next time you put up your prayer...also pray for their parents as well, their strength, and their peace of mind as they rely on God, the ultimate Father, always handling, dealing, watching, and yes, loving, His prodigal children. He too waits for the day when they will be alive again, and no longer lost, but found.

CHAPTER ELEVEN

GIVING TESTIMONY

Seek not the favor of the multitude; it is seldom got by honest and lawful means. But seek the testimony of few; and number not voices, but weigh them.
- Immanuel Kant[1]

It is my sincere hope that if you have read this far into the book, you recognize not all evangelism can take the form of a testimony. We need to think bigger and beyond the immediacy of ourselves in evangelism, and strive to meet the needs of others when evangelizing. It is not my intention, however, to reject testimony all together. I believe testimony can be an important part of evangelism in many instances, especially if it is done with meaning and proper intent. If we give a testimony the right way, testimony can point people to the Lord and enhance what they already know or perceive about Him.

What is testimony?

What we call "testimony" or "giving witness" is usually a re-telling of who we are, where we came from, and how our faith conversion has brought us to a new place from where we started. When one gives "testimony," they may recount a part of their lives or all of it. It may be done as part of a service, as part of an evangelism outreach, or as part of a writing or other program. It is our story as part of the great "cloud of witnesses," spoken from a perspective of where we were, who we are, and where we are going, thanks to the work of God in our lives.

Testimony is not something that, as we discussed earlier, is going to cause the majority of non-believers to fall down at your feet in repentance. It's not a substitute for genuinely learning about one's faith and sharing about it, nor is it a "lazy man's evangelism." When used to encourage, to expound upon, and to enhance faith, testimony is a powerful and effective tool. It must be used in its context for the best results.

Why is testimony important?

Revelation 12:11 says: *"And they overcame him because of the blood of the Lamb and because of the word of their testimony, and they did not love their life even when faced with death."*

Testimony is important because it re-presents the overcoming power of the Lord, pointing to the blood of the Lamb and proving that Jesus is true and His work continues. It shows God's hand still active, present, and relevant in our lives. If God can do it for us, we know – and share – so others know He can do it for them, as well.

Who can give testimony?

There is a definite bias toward testimonies considered more "dramatic," such as those that involve a visible healing or deliverance. These are not the only stories that need to be told, however. Anyone who is a believer has overcome something and has something to share with others. Everyone should be encouraged to give testimony as is applicable in one's life and taught how to apply it properly, as an encouragement and hope, for others.

A good testimony is...

What makes a good testimony? It seems like some testimonies grab our attention, while others put us to sleep. It's more than the details of the testimony that make a testimony effective; it's also the presentation of it. Some pinpoints for a good testimony include:

- **Honest** – If you are making up your testimony as you go along, you will get caught at some point in time. Testimonies should be honest recounts, not interesting fiction narratives. Don't use your testimony as an attempt to try and amaze or impress people.

- **Appropriate for the audience** – Testimony shouldn't be used to hold people captive. Sometimes it's appropriate for longer testimonies; at other times, shorter testimonies are more appropriate. Certain content is inappropriate for youth audiences, while some content is appropriate for all audiences. Make sure the testimony you give is understandable and appropriate to where you give it.

- **Christ-centered** – Testimonies aren't about drawing people unto yourself. It's not about how wonderful you are or what you can do now that you are born again. While the story is from your life, the point of a testimony is to show people God's glory and Christ's saving power in it, not to make yourself sound good or to gain sympathy from others.

- **Purposed** – Telling random stories from your life is not giving testimony. A testimony has a purpose, and that is to prove God faithful through your own experience. How can this purpose come forth as you give testimony?

- **Experienced-based** – We can argue all day long about the Bible and what this verse means and that

165

verse means. What we experience with God, nobody can take from us. Testimony should relate how you have experienced God, not just how you discovered something was true in a doctrinal approach.

Components of a good testimony

Good testimonies are not just aimless ramblings, but are well-constructed. When we see references to testimony in the Bible, it is implied that testimony was to be given with eloquence (Psalm 40:9-10, Psalm 71:15-18, Psalm 119:46). We too should strive to make sure our testimonies contain certain elements and drive home our ultimate point: God has been good to us.

- **Introduce yourself** – Don't assume the audience or individual knows who you are. Let people know your name and why you are giving your testimony.

- **Beginning, middle, and future promise** – In understanding testimony, let's look at testimony as containing three parts: a beginning, middle, and future promise, or conclusion. The beginning of a testimony gives a background of how you got to where you were when you came to know the Lord. Our conversion experience, when Jesus comes into our lives, is the "middle" because it sits at the center of our experience. Coming to Jesus, what He took us through, and where He has brought us to now is a part of this middle experience. Our future promise is where we are heading as we continue to walk with the Lord. It shows that we are continuing to follow where God would have us to go, because we trust in Him.

- **Confession** – If you weren't always saved (none of us were), it's important to be honest about who you were before you were in Christ and the work God has done in your life. Whether it's things that were done to you, things you did, things you did as a result of what was done to you, bad choices, running from God, disobedience, occult or false religious involvement, or anything else – good testimonies admit human weakness. They admit and show the power of God at work in our lives is not of us, and our honesty needs to come through in our testimonies.

- **Clarity** – You lived your life, but others were not there with you. It's important that you are clear in your experiences and, if you are not for some reason, that you explain that your details or memories are fuzzy.

- **Experience of spiritual things** – Discuss encounters you have had with God. Point out the highlights of the ways God has reached out to you, and the wonders that He has worked in your life.

- **Clarify the "why" of your belief** – While testimonies aren't necessarily doctrinal recitations, a testimony should include what it was that made you come to an understanding and belief about the truth of Christianity. What was it that made you come to the realization of the faith? How did faith become such an important facet in your life? How has your faith grown? These are all important aspects to a testimony.

- **Present well** – Dress for the occasion in keeping with what is expected in the atmosphere where you are.

- **Know your audience** – If certain aspects of the faith are important to your audience, or you are part of an event that has a "theme," work your testimony and the elements of it into that theme, while accentuating important aspects. On the same topic but a different note, be careful of the words you use. If you know you are dealing with an audience that is not Christian, avoid using clichés or commonly used terms in church without explaining what they mean.

- **Be relatable** – If you seem distant from your testimony or from your own experience, others are going to have a hard time relating to it. It's important that you are able to connect with your own experience and tell your own story, as it is yours.

- **Have more than one version of your testimony prepared** – I have numerous versions of my testimony, including one longer one and several shorter ones that all relate to specific aspects of my conversion, ministry call, and walk with God. This way, it is easier to relate what is necessary given any situation.

Things to avoid in testimony

- **Droning on...and on...and on...** - Testimony is a balance between not enough information and too much information. It's important to remember that every single detail of your life is not necessary to testimony, and should not be included. Important aspects of one's life (the highlights) are part of a testimony, not every single mundane detail.

- **Bad language or inappropriate content** – There is no reason to use fowl language or suggestive or otherwise inappropriate content in a testimony. The difference between the something inappropriate and something not inappropriate is simple: inappropriate content provides too much detail. For example: It's fine to say that you were sexually involved with someone and she got pregnant. It is not fine to tell us what position you were in when conception occurred. It's fine to say you had a problem with drugs, it is not fine to tell us how to be an intravenous drug user. If you are in doubt about content, discuss the sensitive nature of certain aspects of your testimony with your leader.

- **Be careful of using real names without permission** – Not everyone supports the journey you have made as a believer. Even though everyone was fine with where everyone was once upon a time, that does not mean everyone is fine with it now, in hindsight, or with everyone knowing about it. Protecting privacy – referring to people relationally (father, mother, sister, brother, friend, etc.) without names or changing names may be required for a testimony.

- **Watch the "entertainment factor"** – Yes, people love a good story, but don't give a false testimony in the hopes that people will respond better to your testimony if you "beef" it up. Exaggeration is still dishonest.

- **Thank everyone for giving you the opportunity to share with them** – Testimonies are a conversation: they are one where you speak, the audience listens, the Holy Ghost brings the listeners into a place of spiritual hearing. Thank them for participating in this experience, this journey, with you.

CHAPTER TWELVE

TALKING POINTS FOR EVANGELISM

It is the duty of every Christian to be Christ to his neighbor.
-Martin Luther[1]

Remember in the days before we were saved, how we used to do this cool thing, called talking with other people? We'd say something, and they'd say something, and we'd say something back, and they'd say something back. We'd have this thing with others called a conversation. Nobody felt threatened, offended, angry, or upset, unless you hit a hot-button topic, like politics. We would share. We would listen. We would interact.

What is it about conversion that causes us to be totally devoid of the ability to speak to one another like human beings? Something that used to come so naturally to us suddenly grows into an argument and a shouting match. This is especially true when it comes to evangelism and talking to others about the Lord. Something that should be a blessing and bring joy turns into a battle of wills and ends with people never speaking again. This should not be...but too often, it is.

The best evangelism is a conversation. That means we need to learn how to have them again without anger or attack, but for the benefit of the Kingdom.

Have you learned what you've believed?

I believe most people who want to tell others about the Lord have good motives. They are well-intentioned people who want to share what they have received from God with others. This, unfortunately, isn't enough to make evangelism effective. The secret to the Christian life that's only a secret because we don't talk about it today is that being a Christian is a multi-faceted experience. Being a believer is about a lot more than just attending church on Sunday and trying to get others to see things from your perspective. It's about how you live, how you interact with other people, and how God has transformed your own problems through the power of faith. It is also about knowing how your beliefs relate to practical interactions for everyday life.

So the question of this heading begins: have you learned what you believe? If you don't understand your own beliefs and how those apply to your own life, change, and witness, you are going to have a hard time trying to talk to anyone else about them. It's important you have at least some idea of why you are where you are in your life. Why do you believe in God? How has becoming a Christian changed your life? What challenges do you face, and how do you overcome them? How does God help you through what you go through on a regular basis? These are all good questions to start with as you prepare yourself to talk to others about the Lord.

Having things in common

I have nothing against Christian music, movies, or television channels. I do have something against using these things as an excuse to be out of touch with things in society. Being a Christian is not an excuse to hide from the world. We are still people, and we still have interests, thoughts, and ideas that are our own. This also means that we have the right to pursue various activities, enjoy a song or a show, and not constantly worry that any entertainment means will lead us away from salvation. (On a side note: when selecting activities, what you pick is up to your discretion. I am not advocating activities or programming that is somehow immoral or spiritually offensive.

In keeping with this, do not judge the things your brother or sister in the faith may select that is different from yours.)

There is another reason, however, why the Christian's life needs to be bigger than a few low-budget Christian-themed movies and songs. Watching television, movies, listening to secular music, having hobbies (cooking, hiking, exercise, reading, writing, etc.), and having diverse interests also gives us common ground when speaking to other people. It's very difficult to have a conversation with someone if the only thing we can talk about is a movie that nobody went to see or favorite Bible verses when the person we are talking to has no reference for conversation. We need to be able to talk to people about just about anything that can help build a level of reference and interaction. This helps people to feel like they are a part of the discussion, not just being lectured about points of belief. It also shows that you are interested in the world around you. Christians today have a reputation for being only about the things that interest them, so being someone who is well-rounded and knowledgeable about different things shows others that what you have to say is relevant and informed.

Be relevant and informed

I just mentioned being knowledgeable about things in the last section. Here I am mentioning it all by itself because I think it's an important principle. Too often Christians use nothing more than "Christian" news outlets or "Christian" themed political venues as their sources for information. Time and time again, these "sources" have been proven to promote false, misleading, or biased in their reporting. Spouting off facts from these limited sources shows that not only is your faith irrelevant, you aren't making a point to be informed about the essential issues of the day. It is my personal preference to avoid discussions relating to politics, but if you want to talk politics, you need to talk politics from an informed viewpoint. If you want to talk faith, you need to talk about it from a relevant viewpoint. Be a part of things! Don't talk or engage others with of recycled information...talk as one who has made a point to be informed on matters rather than just opinionated.

Be interested in others

Evangelism doesn't follow a script. There is no way you can know where a discussion might take you or what you might have to answer. The essential nature of evangelism is coming to a place where you talk to someone so you can offer them the truth of the Lord, and they will become a disciple of His. We know the answer is Christ, but the process to get to that answer is not the same for everyone. That is why being interested in other people is so essential. You don't know how to reach out to somebody else if you don't know what they are looking for, what is important to them, or where they feel they need to be. Being a person who is genuinely interested in others – listening when they speak, paying attention when they have something to offer – reaching out with care when they need it – is an essential part of evangelism. This lets people know that God cares and knows of them in a personal way, listening and attending to the issues they have. People need to be treated like they are people, with individual issues, ideas, and thoughts, and not just as another head to count in church attendance.

It's not what you say, it's how you say it

I've already addressed the issue of the offensive church in the chapter on church hurt. I will reiterate again: we, as Christians, need to be careful with what comes out of our mouths. We are quick to say that people misjudge us, but is that really the case? Are people miss-assessing us based on what we said, or is it something in how we said it?

It is often not what we have to say that is offensive, but how we say it. Below I am going to display different ways something can be said and how different they can clearly sound to the hearer:

- "Why was the door locked?"
- "Why did you lock me out?"

- "Where is the milk?"
- "What did you do with the milk?"

- "I'm not having a good day."
- "Nothing ever goes right for me."

The different statements above describe the same incidents, but spoken two different ways. The first way states whatever is going on in a factual way, the second in an accusatory way. How something is stated can make the difference in the acceptance of a statement, or its total rejection.

We need to pay attention to how we use our words and what message we convey with them, especially in Gospel proclamation. People can hear they are miserable, useless, and unacceptable to God, or they can hear that they are loved by God despite the things they have done in their lives. Either way, the message we give them is very much up to us and our words.

Think of it like this: what kind of a message do you want to receive about something? Does it matter how that message is conveyed to you? Of course it matters how we receive our messages, whatever they may be. In evangelism, you are giving people the best news imaginable about life and hope. Every problem, every situation, everything they face has an answer in Christ. So why is it that we use this as an opportunity to brow-beat people into conversion?

Spirit-led evangelism

Spirit-led evangelism is the opposite of strategic evangelistic moves often made by people who want to reach as many people as possible in evangelism. Spirit-led evangelism may very well mean that you don't reach out to fifty people in a session, but it does mean that the evangelism has a deeper and more effective impact.

We need to do evangelism from a Spirit-led perspective because after so many years, I have yet to meet anyone – myself included – who was ever converted by reading a tract or watching a Christian movie. While it sounds great that these things will seemingly reach a lot of people, it isn't working the way we hope it will. We need to put the Spirit at the forefront of what we do, for we know it is the Spirit that leads us into all truth.

In Spirit-led evangelism, you let the Spirit guide you who to talk to, what to talk about, and how to discuss it. Each situation may very well be different, but every situation is Spirit-led, leading you to that individual and their specific needs. To operate proper Spirit-led evangelism, do the following:

- **Pray beforehand** – Start praying to be led to individuals and have individuals led to you at least one day beforehand. Ask the Lord to open your heart, your mouth, and your mind to those you will be meeting and the different circumstances they are facing.

- **Be people-minded** – The purpose of evangelism is to reach other people. Be friendly, be outgoing, be kind. Start conversations based on a compliment (what someone is wearing) and strike up a conversation about something non-threatening and non-offensive. Listen to what is important to them and what they are looking for in their lives.

- **Don't expect people to fall in a big heap at your feet in conversion** – This only happens in cheaply made Christian movies; it does not happen in real life. Conversion can be a process in many people of moving toward God and away from other things. Don't expect immediate, instant results; plant seeds.

- **Ask the Lord for the word of knowledge and the word of wisdom to activate in the process** – Many people need a word from God, even if they don't realize it. They need God to move on their behalf and need to know that God cares about what they are going through. A word of knowledge or a word of wisdom is the perfect way to tap into whatever is going on in their lives from a spiritual perspective.

- **Let people express themselves** – People have questions, thoughts, feelings, and ideas that come up in the natural course of conversation. A conversation that is God-based should be no different! Let people express themselves and their thoughts, within the bounds of respect and honesty.

- **Talk about whatever God lays on your heart** – Don't try to restrict the Gospel to a script. When Jesus spoke before crowds, He didn't have a bunch of notes in front of Him. He didn't spend His childhood memorizing the words He would speak as an adult. Don't make it so rehearsed! There are so many different things you can talk about that will be truly good news for many...say them!

- **Avoid the temptation to be "preachy"** – If someone wants to be preached to, they will go to a church service. They don't need to feel like you are preaching to them, they need to feel like you are talking to them as a human being about something important. Along the same lines, avoid controversial, hot-button issues. This is not the time for people to feel judged.

CHAPTER THIRTEEN

QUESTIONS AND ANSWERS FOR POTENTIAL AND NEW DISCIPLES

Someone asked, Will the heathen who have never heard the Gospel be saved? It is more a question with me whether we -- who have the Gospel and fail to give it to those who have not -- can be saved.
- Charles Spurgeon[1]

New disciples and potential new disciples tend to have a lot of questions about faith. This is normal and to be expected. The only time it is problematic is when we, as leaders and those who have been disciples for an extended period of time, are not expedient to answer the questions of the new disciples. Having been in a situation where I am trying to answer the questions of a new disciple, I know how challenging it can be as question leads to question. I also know many questions of new believers are similar. In this chapter, I am going to go over some of the questions new disciples have – and good answers for them.

Why should I believe in God?

I understand why this question is asked, but maybe this question needs to be answered with another question: why shouldn't you believe in God? There are so many different ways people argue this question. I could take you to a bunch of Bible verses, but the truth is that if you have questions about believing in God to begin with, trying to prove God with a book you are already unsure about is not going to answer the question in a way you are looking for.

I'm also not going to answer this question with a lot of "proofs" that people tend to rely on. I do not discount the various scientific facts and data that enhances the defense of God's existence, but I believe that when people are asking as to why they should believe in God, they are looking for a more practical, personal approach to the question.

The simplest reason why we should believe in God is because every culture of the world, every nation that has ever lived, has sought to find and connect with its Creator. There is no question that, along the way, people imposed their own viewpoints therein and did not always properly understand God Himself, but the fact that every culture, everywhere in the world, acknowledges that something greater than human life began this planet and maintains it has to be relevant in our understanding and acceptance of God in our own lives. This search for the divine, for something higher than humanity, has existed since time began.

For people to be seeking something generation after generation for thousands of years would be totally illogical if that "something" did not exist. If you are reaching out, questioning why you should believe in God, that is the very reason why you should believe, seek His face, and look more deeply into His existence.

Believing in God is a matter of faith. It is accepting the reality that people have sought God for thousands of years and have always stood upon the principle that if they seek Him, they will gain the revelation they seek. There have been studies that prove believing in God is good for one's life, health, and outlook on life throughout the journey. It helps us weather difficulties and rejoice in the good times. You should believe in God because He does exist, He cares about you, and desires that you know Him unto the end of eternal life with Him.

Why does it matter which god I believe in?

It's a wonderful, idealistic attitude to believe that all paths lead to God and everything in the world is an extension of the same idea. It sounds romantic and fairy-tale like to assume everything is like everything else. The reality, however, is that this is simply not true. It matters which god you believe in because not every god is true. While I certainly acknowledge that every religion has things in common, those commonalities do not override the differences of religious groups. If we are going to believe in God, we need to believe in the truth about Him, because He desires that we would find Him as He is. If we are to have a relationship with Him, it would be contrary for us to chase and pursue an alternate god because we think they are all the same. Choosing to believe in and follow God means we choose to follow the true God, and learn all about Him in keeping with His revelation to us.

If God exists, why is there suffering, wars, etc.?

God, as the Creator of the world, governs the world as He will. The way He has chosen to govern humanity is through the principle of free will. God has given each one of us the right to decide what we will do, in each and every situation, once we are at a place in our lives where we can decide what we will do. Suffering in this world, wars, etc. are all a result of the consequences of sin – that people willingly choose to do things that are wrong and those things affect other people negatively. God wants to be our choice, and He wants us to follow Him of our own choosing. Suffering and wars exist because people do not obey the will of God. If they were to do this, things would be different.

What can Christianity offer me that something else can't?

The opportunity to come into a relationship with God through Jesus Christ, thus to become a part of a life and experience that is truly eternal.

What must I do to be saved?

This is the million-dollar question, isn't it? When people came and asked Jesus this question, He answered it in more than one way. Most often, Jesus answered this question by addressing people's hearts and the issues that were often keeping them far away from truly becoming a disciple of the Lord. If we study the New Testament, we learn there are four different aspects of becoming a believer:

- **Believe** – You cannot be a Christian if you do not believe in God and you do not believe in Jesus.

- **Repent** – You must understand that you have done things in life that offend God and desire to turn around from those ways, and start living according to the precepts of God.

- **Be baptized** – A water baptism, in full immersion, in the Name of the Father, Son, and Holy Spirit, and the Name of Jesus Christ, for the remission of sins. This does not "save" you, but it unites you to Christ in His death.

- **Confess** – In confession, you verbally acknowledge that you are accepting the governance of God, and Jesus Christ is the Lord of your life.

Which Bible translation is the best?

Any time you are reading a translation of the Bible, you are reading just that – a translation. Since the Reformation, the purpose of Bible translations is to help the average person read the Bible in a language they will understand. For this reason, there are many different translations available to suit different audiences and needs of the reader. There isn't a "best" Bible translation, although some are more accurate than others; there are different translations intended to assist different audiences and levels of understanding. Selecting a

Bible translation is, therefore, something based on what you are seeking as an individual who is looking to study the Word. There are paraphrases (when the text is written not for authenticity or accuracy, but readability), reference and study Bibles (written for people who want to take a more scholarly or doctrinal approach to the Word), interlinear studies (where the original text is literally translated into English), word-for-word translations (where the Bible is translated literally word-for-word), and thought-for-thought translations (where the Bible is translated to capture the essence of thoughts rather than literal word renderings). It is my recommendation that every serious student of the Bible have at least one version of each type of translation available for cross-reference study.

How can I trust the Bible?

The Bible is a revelation of God. It is an inspired record of the ways God has revealed and interacted with people throughout salvation history. Because it is a revelation of God, we can know – and trust – God has given it to us for our own enlightenment and edification.

How do I select the right church for me?

I believe that yes, while in the natural realm we may "select" a church for ourselves, God draws us to where we should be, and when. As believers, it is vitally important we open ourselves to the leading of the Spirit, so we can be where God desires us to learn and gain our necessary foundations of faith. When you are in the right place, you will know. That is as deep as I can get on that answer.

How should I pray?

Prayer is a form of communication with God. The Word tells us we are to *"Pray without ceasing"* (1 Thessalonians 5:17). We pray whenever we are speaking to God. Prayer can be public (done in an assembly, such as a church), private (done at home, when one is by themselves), verbal (spoken out loud) or done silently (in one's thoughts). In Luke 11:2-4, Jesus tells us how to pray:

And He said to them, "When you pray, say: 'Father, hallowed be Your Name. Your kingdom come. 'Give us each day our daily bread. 'And forgive us our sins, For we ourselves also forgive everyone who is indebted to us. And lead us not into temptation.'"

From these two verses, we can understand how we should interact with God:

- Honor His Name
- Herald and believe in His Kingdom
- Ask for our needs
- Ask for forgiveness of sins
- Forgive others
- Ask to avoid falling into temptation

However you want to do this, in whatever order, is truly your own discretion. The important thing is to talk to God, interact with Him, and allow Him to enhance your life through prayer.

CHAPTER FOURTEEN

THE TOP TEN GRIPES NON-BELIEVERS HAVE WITH CHRISTIANITY

I want Jesus to come back and say, 'THATS NOT WHAT I MEANT!'
— Margaret Cho[1]

I compiled this list based on discussions I have had with various non-Christian individuals. The thing that was most amazing to me was how parallel all the various "gripes" were to one another. Over and over again, I heard the same arguments against Christianity.

The thing that I believe is hardest for us to accept is that the accusations people make about Christians are, very often, quite true. They may not be true about specific Christian individuals, but if one is looking at the whole of Christianity from the outset, the issues non-believers raised to me are valid.

There is an important finding in all of this, however. What Christians need to step back and realize is the majority of non-believers do not refrain from exploring Christianity deeper because they have a problem with Christ or the teachings of Christ. The universal issue people have with Christianity is...Christians.

This means we can do something about it. If someone

has a genuine gripe with Jesus, we can sit and argue that with them all day, but it is much harder to try and fix that issue. If the problem is Christians, we can look closer at what we need to change and change our behavior.

1. Christians are narrow-minded

If we do a survey of Christians today, most keep themselves at a distance from the world. They are very preoccupied with their families, their churches, and do not venture far from their immediate fold for any reason whatsoever. Exploring the world, different beliefs, and having different ideas on anything (even things that have nothing to do with the Bible or faith) is regarded as forbidden.

Christians also tend to preoccupy themselves with issues that nobody in the larger world care about: women's ordination, infant baptism, whether or not women can wear pants or make-up, who should work in a household, and other things like this...but with a focus so overblown on such matters, is it any wonder the world is turned off?

- **Ways we can combat this:** Watch the arguments online, in public, and in forums where non-believers may be watching. Expand life outside of your immediate communities; make friends with different types of people; and stop endlessly debating issues that have been debated to death.

2. Christians do not embrace scholarship

In my own journey, this was probably one of the biggest hurdles I had to overcome. Being an academic (by the time I converted, I was already in college and working on a more advanced degree), I found the lack of scholarship in church to be disappointing. We did not speak of church history, we did not consider the vast number of believers who had gone on before us, and while we were people who were quick to defend what we felt was right from a medical or a scientific perspective, those perspectives seemed to me to be so uninformed. It just sounded like we were picking out what we liked the best based on whoever told us it appeared to be Biblical.

There has been a large exodus of Protestant and non-denominational ministers out of their respective churches and into more traditional denominations, such as Roman Catholicism, Orthodox Catholicism, and high Anglicanism due to the lack of scholarship in our modern churches. When such educated scholars seek more from their faith and deeper teaching, they often are unable to find it in their respective churches of origin or ordination.

The modern Christian movement has long had its issues with education and secular society. Many Christian groups avoid scholarship on the same basis as their ancestors did, and that is fear that education will take them away from the faith. The result of this anti-educational stance is a departure from the faith on the part of those who desire to see their faith from a scholarly perspective.

- **Ways we can combat this:** Christianity, despite the denomination, needs to embrace and understand its history. We need to realize that while education may change the perspective we have on a specific issue, it is not going to cause us to depart and rebel against our faith. We need to make room for people of all educational backgrounds, including scholars. Christians should aspire to attend or even start seminaries, Bible schools, and pursue educational aspects of Christianity.

3. Christians are judgmental

This is a controversial one...but are people wrong for thinking this? I have known one too many Christians who felt they had the right to tell me or somebody else what was right, based on nothing more than their opinion of a situation. I felt looked down upon, criticized, and like I was never going to be "good enough."

Whether we intend to convey this or not, this is exactly how people feel when they feel judged. Things aren't always the way they look or appear on the outside and yes, it may be convenient to just jump to a conclusion without listening or considering all the facts, there is always a story behind someone's situation. If we aren't going to offer them an avenue out, we need to keep ourselves in check.

- **Ways we can combat this:** There is a difference between what is right as a moral stance and dealing with a human being who is in a situation that may very well be morally offensive to someone. Jesus has called us to be a people of salt and light, bearing truth wherever we go. You don't have to agree with what someone is doing, but you also don't have to make that known at every single turn and opportunity. Be there when people are ready, and in the meantime, love them enough to help them through what they are going through.

4. Christians are hypocrites

Christians talk about love, then talk about hating the Muslim neighbor they have. They talk about being in favor of life, and then support capital punishment. They say that hate is wrong, and then they say they hate their gay son or daughter. They say they want to be people who impact the world, and then spend seven days a week at church. Every day, it seems we hear about Christians who claim one thing, but do something very, very different from what they claim.

Not all Christians are hypocrites, just as not all Christians are guilty of the things on this list. Once again, however, the fact that many people give the impression of Christian hypocrisy means non-believers just assume all Christians are the same way about matters.

- **Ways we can combat this:** It is very vital that Christians live according to the beliefs they profess. If you are a Christian, you need to examine your actions, and realize people are watching. If they don't match up with what you claim to believe, your actions need to change.

5. Christians are intolerant

There is a general understanding among many Christian circles today that disagreement equates to a right to be downright cruel and intolerant of other people. They feel that disagreement with a homosexual orientation gives one the right to berate, harass, bully, or reject gays and lesbians. Those who are divorced are often seen as outsiders who didn't try hard enough to make their marriages work. Women who are single parents aren't doing a good enough job. Then there is the whole issue of racism in the church, which many either want to pretend doesn't exist or don't want to hear about it when it does come up.

Today's Christians are also very defensive of what they deem "traditional values," when many of them roared through the 1960s, 70s, 80s, and 90s, living with people they were not married to, doing drugs, having sex, and doing whatever they wanted in the meantime.

Even though many Christians did all the same things that people do now, they look on others who do them. Not considering a world full of temptations that they themselves also have succumbed to at different points in time, Christians gain a general intolerance to anyone and anything that challenges them or looks different from them.

- **Ways we can combat this:** It's time to stop using faith as an excuse to be a bigot. You don't have to agree with someone to love them. You do not have any right to stand in the place of God, deeming a race or group of people inferior, bullying people, or judging someone as worthy of mistreatment. This stops with education, with truth, and when we let God stand as judge of people instead of us ourselves.

6. Christians are arrogant

If you watch online, the vast number of Christians on social networks display the following behaviors:

- Nasty attitudes
- Deliberately posting things that are not only controversial, they are controversial to the point of being offensive
- Quick to get angry and hostile when someone disagrees with them

Arrogance is a state of being whereby someone thinks they are superior to everyone else. This manifests in a number of ways, obviously, but if one thinks themselves superior, it's not a big leap of faith to consider they also regard their opinions, perspectives, and thoughts superior to everyone else's, as well. The way in which too many Christians carry themselves gives off a clear air of arrogance, thinking what they have to say and what they think is the end all, be all in every situation.

- **Ways we can combat this:** Stop being arrogant! Let other people have their opinions and perspectives. It's fine to demand everyone remain respectful, but stop demanding everyone else agrees with you. Turn down the attitude. Not every opinion, thought, or perspective you have falls within the category of being "true" or "Biblical;" some things are just thoughts and opinions...so take a deep breath...and let someone else have a thought, feeling, and opinion.

7. Christians are intrusive

When someone asks you personal questions, interferes in your life without warrant, or starts assuming you are doing certain things without facts, how do you feel? How does it feel to be asked questions, such as:

- "Are you having sex with your boyfriend/girlfriend?"
- "Are you and your spouse having marital troubles?"
- "Are you having issues with your children?"
- "Why do you want to eat that?"
- "Why do you think that?
- "Why do you want that?"

- "Why do you believe that?"

Asking such questions isn't done because one fears for another's salvation, but to be nosy. Is it any wonder that people get annoyed with Christians?

I'm going to say this and risk making some Christians very annoyed: Some things are just not your business. You do not need to know every detail of everyone's life in order to bless someone else and bring them to a place of love and salvation in their lives.

- **Ways we can combat this:** Mind your own business. Don't use the Gospel as an excuse to be nosy.

8. Christians do not reflect the character or teachings of Christ

Granted there is considerable disagreement about how to interpret Christ's words, there are some commands of Christ that aren't debatable: loving your neighbor as yourself, serving others, being good to people, and having solid character are some that come to mind. In a prosperity-hungry church, it can seem like values of selflessness and honoring others falls by the wayside in favor of financial gain and selfishness.

- **Ways we can combat this:** Do what Jesus told you to do! Get out there, serve others, be minded toward assisting others, stop being so much about self, and stop being so much about money.

9. Christians are always making assumptions about others

Not long ago, I shared a link about a popular news media issue on Facebook. Someone who was on my friends' list at the time responded in a negative and sarcastic manner. At first, those who were commenting on the post ignored her. When it was obvious she was not getting the response she wanted, she accused everyone in the discussion who disagreed with her of not really being saved. This is just one example of how a so-called "believer" judged in this instance other believers based on an opinion. Now, think about how many assumptions are made about non-believers? How many times have you gotten into a debate with someone else and either been assumed to be a certain way or assumed someone else to be a certain way?

- **Ways we can combat this:** Refrain from being so free with opinions, observations, and assessments of others. Never drop an assumption in casual conversation, because not only does such cause offense, it also causes people to be uninterested in what you have to say.

10. Christians are unforgiving

This accusation is akin to hypocrisy in many ways, because the basic message of Christianity is God's love and forgiveness of humanity through Jesus Christ. It is a little more personalized, however, because to the world, Christians seem angry and aggressive. They seem unrelenting, unwilling to give people the benefit of the doubt, and unwilling to exercise mercy. The world sees this as a group of people who don't follow their own precepts and don't adhere to their own Gospel.

- **Ways we can combat this:** Since our own attitudes of unforgiveness nullify what we proclaim to be Gospel, we can do what God commands and forgive others. It does not mean we have to entertain everyone or want to have a relationship with everyone who has wronged us, but it does mean that we stop harboring the wrongs done to us from the past.

CHAPTER FIFTEEN

TWELVE-WEEK NEW DISCIPLES CLASS

*We Christians are debtors to all men at all times in all places,
but we are so smug to the lostness of men. We've been "living
in Laodicea ", lax, loose, lustful, and lazy. Why is there this criminal
indifference to the lostness of men? Our condemnation is that
we know how to live better than we are living.*
- Leonard Ravenhill[1]

ere I am outlining the major points for a twelve-week
New Disciples Class. A class of this sort should be
made available at least once or twice per year in each
church for potential new members and curious
"onlookers" or "seekers" who seek to learn more about their
faith and possibly join the church in pursuit of discipleship.

The goal of this class is three-fold:

- To provide information about the faith
- To prepare candidates to receive the ordinance of baptism
- To establish a solid foundation for discipleship and fellowship that will last

Classes should be done according to the needs of the

community: on a weeknight or as a weekend day-seminar, whatever is most appropriate. Class topics can be drawn out and turned into day sessions, or can be held for two-to-three hours on a weeknight.

I am providing an outline without specified notes because I recognize each church may have different needs when it comes to these classes. While certain information is universal, certain aspects of the class, the verses or Bible translation used, and the way information may be presented may vary depending on the needs present.

Week 1: Who Is God?

1. God in the Old Testament
    a. God in Creation
    b. God calls Abram
    c. God with Moses and through the Exodus
    d. The implementation of the Law

2. God through Jesus Christ in the New Testament
    a. Fall of mankind equates to sin in the world
    b. The Law given to make us aware of sin
    c. God provides us an answer through salvation

3. Preparing for and making baptism available to candidates
    a. What baptism is
    b. What baptism signifies
    c. Why baptism is important
    d. How – and why – we are baptized

Week 2: God In Experience: The Holy Ghost/Spirit

1. Studying the gifts (*charisma*) given to the church for the edification of the Body
    a. Word of wisdom
    b. Word of knowledge
    c. Healing
    d. Miracles
    e. Discernment of spirits

    f. Speaking in tongues
    g. Interpreting tongues
    h. Prophecy
    i. Faith
    j. Service
    k. Teaching
    l. Exhortation
    m. Giving
    n. Leadership
    o. Mercy

2. Leadership (*didomi*) gifts
    a. Apostles
    b. Prophets
    c. Evangelists
    d. Pastors
    e. Teachers

3. What it means to be called and chosen for ministry
    a. Being called for ministry is different than serving in a leadership position in church for a period of time
    b. The blessings and challenges of having a calling
    c. What ministering leaders do for you
    d. Why it is important to honor and submit to leadership

4. The fruit of the Spirit
    a. Love
    b. Joy
    c. Peace
    d. Patience
    e. Kindness
    f. Goodness
    g. Faithfulness
    h. Gentleness (humility)
    i. Self-control

Week 3: Holy Living

1. What it means to be holy (set apart)
   a. Being a part of the Kingdom of God
   b. The difference between the Kingdom and the world

2. Self-governance
   a. Getting right with God
   b. Loving God before all things
   c. Loving your neighbor as yourself
   d. Personal conduct
   e. Integrity

3. Being a part of a family
   a. Single life
   b. Married life
   c. Parents and children

4. Being part of the church
   a. Membership
   b. Submission to leaders
   c. Offering gifts
   d. Participation

5. Being part of society
   a. Submission to governmental authority
   b. Being a good employee or a good employer
   c. Serving the community

Week 4: Christian Service

1. Membership and participation in church
   a. Your church needs you!
   b. Attendance
   c. Special events
   d. Ways you can be more involved

2. Stewardship
   a. What it means to be a "good steward"

       b. Time management

       c. Managing resources

       d. Respecting God's creation

3. Financial giving
    a. Tithes
    b. Offerings
    c. Special giving

4. Giving of time
    a. Volunteering
    b. Being of service
    c. Looking for opportunities to serve

Week 5: Christian Rites, Rituals, And Ordinances

1. Why God has established rites, rituals, and ordinances for us as believers
    a. To celebrate our growth in Him
    b. To unite us as a Body
    c. To honor God's sacred presence in our lives

2. The Rites
    a. Ordination
    b. Appointments
    c. Weddings
    d. Funerals

3. Rituals
    a. Presentations/Dedications
    b. Consecration
    c. Anointing

4. Ordinances
    a. Baptism
    b. Communion

Week 6: Introduction To The Word I

1. Studying the Word

a. What do you seek to get out of the Word?
b. Rightly dividing the Word
c. Receiving revelation from the Word
d. Understanding the Word
e. Hearing God speak to us from the Word

2. Devotional reading
   a. Reading the Word as a daily practice
   b. Learning to meditate on the Word

3. Study tools for Bible study
   a. Bible atlas
   b. Concordance
   c. Bible dictionary

4. Understanding what it means to have and believe in an inspired Word
   a. Trusting God's revelation in the Word
   b. Understanding interpretation and translation
   c. Seeing the Word apply in our lives and times
   d. Hearing the Word on a regular basis
   e. Understanding *Logos* (written, personal, and expressed word) and *Rhema* (revelatory word)

Week 7: Introduction To The Word II

1. The Old Testament
   a. The Torah/Pentateuch (Law)
      i. Genesis
      ii. Exodus
      iii. Leviticus
      iv. Numbers
      v. Deuteronomy
   b. Historical Books
      i. Joshua
      ii. Judges
      iii. Ruth
      iv. 1 Samuel
      v. 2 Samuel

        vi. 1 Kings
        vii. 2 Kings
        viii. 1 Chronicles
        ix. 2 Chronicles
        x. Ezra
        xi. Nehemiah
  c. The Poetry and Wisdom Writings
        i. Job
        ii. Psalms
        iii. Proverbs
        iv. Ecclesiastes
        v. Song of Songs
  d. The Prophets
        i. Isaiah
        ii. Jeremiah
        iii. Lamentations
        iv. Ezekiel
        v. Daniel
        vi. Hosea
        vii. Joel
        viii. Amos
        ix. Obadiah
        x. Jonah
        xi. Micah
        xii. Nahum
        xiii. Habakkuk
        xiv. Zephaniah
        xv. Haggai
        xvi. Zechariah
        xvii. Malachi

2. The New Testament
  a. The Synoptic Gospels
        i. Matthew
        ii. Mark
        iii. Luke
  b. Acts of the Apostles
  c. The Pauline Letters
        i. Romans
        ii. 1 Corinthians

     iii. 2 Corinthians
     iv. Galatians
     v. Ephesians
     vi. Philippians
     vii. Colossians
     viii. 1 Thessalonians
     ix. 2 Thessalonians
     x. 1 Timothy
     xi. 2 Timothy
     xii. Titus
     xiii. Philemon
   d. The Petrine Epistles
     i. 1 Peter
     ii. 2 Peter
   e. The General Epistles
     i. Hebrews
     ii. James
     iii. Jude
   f. The Writings of John
     i. John
     ii. 1 John
     iii. 2 John
     iv. 3 John
     v. Revelation

Week 8: The Spiritual Life

1. The grace of God
 a. How grace and faith work together
 b. How the grace of God manifests in our lives
 c. Why grace is important
 d. Grace and forgiveness
 e. How to apply forgiveness in our own lives

2. What it means to be a part of the Kingdom of God
 a. How kingdoms function
 b. Kingdom government and government
  officials
 c. Life for a kingdom citizen
 d. Privileges for kingdom citizens

e. Requirements for remaining in the Kingdom
　　　　of God
　　　f. What it means that the "Kingdom of God is
　　　　within you"
　　　g. Kingdom principles

　3. Having a relationship with God
　　　a. Understanding God as Father
　　　　　i. The love God has for each of us
　　　　　ii. Receiving the love of God in our lives
　　　　　iii. Understanding sin and how it
　　　　　　　hampers our relationship with God
　　　　　iv. The importance of repentance
　　　　　v. Receiving healing, hope, and
　　　　　　　changing our lives
　　　　　vi. Making better choices through faith
　　　b. Understanding God's guidance
　　　　　i. The "still, small voice"
　　　　　ii. The word of wisdom, word of
　　　　　　　knowledge, and prophecy in your
　　　　　　　own life
　　　　　iii. Gaining a spiritual perspective
　　　　　iv. Applying spiritual principles to
　　　　　　　everyday life
　　　　　v. When God is silent...

Week 9: Growing In God

　1. Moving beyond things elementary
　　　a. God's will for us to develop and grow in the
　　　　faith
　　　b. It is not God's will for us to remain at the
　　　　"basics" forever
　　　c. As we grow we gain deeper spiritual
　　　　perspective

　2. "Spiritual agriculture"
　　　a. Times and seasons
　　　b. Seed-time and harvest
　　　c. Sowing and reaping

d. Abiding in the vine

e. Bearing good fruit

3. Maturity in the faith

   a. Honesty and integrity

   b. Developing good Christian character

   c. Being a Christian in one's everyday life

   d. Church disciplinary measures

4. Fellowship

   a. Interacting with other believers

   b. The need for prayer and praise

   c. Sharing in the life of the Spirit through church unity

Week 10: Christian Disciplines

1. Prayer

   a. What prayer is

   b. How to pray

   c. How prayer changes your life

2. Confessing our sins and faults

   a. The principle of admitting to faults, sins, and failings

   b. Why confession can be a good thing

   c. Understanding this precept in a balanced perspective

3. Fasting

   a. What fasting is

   b. Different ways fasting can apply to one's life

   c. Purposes for fasting

   d. Guidelines for fasting

4. Spiritual warfare

   a. What spiritual warfare is

   b. How spiritual warfare affects the life of a believer

   c. Putting on the whole armor of God

        d. Deliverance ministry

    5. Think on these things
        a. How our words and thoughts affect our
            spiritual lives
        b. Honorable
        c. Right
        d. Pure
        e. Lovely
        f. Of good repute
        g. Excellent
        h. Praiseworthy

Week 11: Discernment

    1. Understanding what discernment is
        a. How discernment is important for our spiritual
            lives
        b. How we tell between different things,
            especially right and wrong
        c. False prophets, teachers, and leaders in the
            church
        d. Looking at what makes a false prophecy,
            teaching, or word

    2. Recognizing the times
        a. What it means to be living in the "last days"
        b. What are "signs of the times?"
        c. How we, as believers, endure
        d. What should we do in these times?

    3. Growing in what's true
        a. How to identify spiritual truth
        b. Avoiding temptations
        c. Avoiding false teachings

    4. Church unity
        a. Uniting with what is true, and away from what
            is false

b. How the Spirit works in the unity of the church
c. Recognizing true leadership and true fellowship
d. What it means to have "all things in common"
e. The universal church beyond the local church

Week 12: Sharing Our Faith With Others

1. Sharing Jesus
    a. Knowing who Jesus is to you
    b. Talking points for evangelism
    c. Presenting Jesus to others
    d. Preparing to give testimony

2. Actions speak louder than words
    a. Maintaining a Christian lifestyle
    b. Witnessing with actions
    c. Showing others that you care and love them as people
    d. Living the faith

CHAPTER SIXTEEN

SIX-WEEK EVANGELISM CLASS

In the vast plain to the north I have sometimes seen, in the morning sun, the smoke of a thousand villages where no missionary has ever been.
- Robert Moffat[1]

For the last chapter of this book, I am outlining the major points for a six-week Evangelism Class. As we've discussed in this book, becoming a successful witness requires more than just arming people with a testimony and sending them out. We need to make sure those who engage in evangelism are properly prepared and armed to go out and represent their faith well. That is who this class is for.

For this class, you can use this text as a starting point, and the class outline as a general guideline for structure and discussion. Anyone in church who desires to share their faith better should be welcome.

The goal of this class is two-fold:

- To provide a forum and foundation to share one's faith with others
- To prepare individuals for evangelistic service

Classes should be done according to the needs of the

community: on a weeknight or as a weekend day-seminar, whatever is most appropriate. Class topics can be drawn out and turned into day sessions, or can be held for two-to-three hours on a weeknight.

I am providing an outline without specified notes because I recognize each church may have different needs when it comes to these classes. While certain information is universal, certain aspects of the class, the verses or Bible translation used, and the way information may be presented may vary depending on the needs present.

Week 1: Who Is Jesus To You?

1. Understanding Jesus in your own life
   a. Who Jesus is
   b. What Jesus did for us
   c. The work of salvation
   d. The resurrection

2. The work of Jesus within you
   a. The teachings of Jesus
   b. The witness of Jesus
   c. The leadership of Jesus
   d. The evangelism of Jesus

3. The role of the Spirit in evangelism
   a. Empowering us to be witnesses
   b. Bringing us into all truth
   c. Conviction
   d. Giving us gifts for the benefit of the Body

Week 2: Talking Points For Evangelism

1. Understanding what evangelism is and why it is so important

2. How to start a conversation
   a. Things in common
   b. Being a diverse people
   c. Respecting differences

        d. Learning about other people

  3. Listening
        a. Being attentive to the needs of others
        b. Showing interest
        c. Giving a word in due season

  4. Discussing God
        a. Handling "uncomfortable points"
        b. Answering questions
        c. Discussing God with people of different religions
        d. Keeping things "Christ-centered"

Week 3: Evangelistic Presentation

  1. Going into "all the world"

  2. The principle of soul-winning
        a. Why we are called to be wise
        b. How we can best pay attention and reach out
        c. Relating to others
        d. Handling the Gospel well

  3. God as relational to humanity
        a. Types and shadows
        b. Personality
        c. Experience
        d. Spiritual gifts
        e. Revelation from the Word
        f. Worship and Praise
        g. Prayer
        h. Miracles

Week 4: Giving Testimony

  1. What is testimony?
        a. Why testimony is important
        b. The center of our testimony, Christ

2. What makes a good testimony?
   a. Honest
   b. Appropriate for the audience
   c. Christ-centered
   d. Purposed
   e. Experienced-based

3. Giving Testimony
   a. Introduce yourself
   b. Beginning, middle, and future promise
   c. Confession
   d. Clarity
   e. Experience of spiritual things
   f. Clarify the "why" of your belief
   g. Present well
   h. Know your audience
   i. Be relatable
   j. Have more than one testimony prepared

4. Things to avoid in testimony
   a. Droning on...and on...and on...
   b. Bad language or inappropriate content
   c. Be careful of using real names without permission
   d. Watch the "entertainment factor"
   e. Thank everyone for giving you the opportunity to share with them

Week 5: Having Things In Common

1. Finding common ground
   a. Avoid preaching "at people"
   b. Understanding judgment and why it is a deal-breaker in evangelism
   c. The importance of discussion
   d. Humility in evangelism
   e. Avoiding the temptation to bully people into the Gospel

2. Idolatry and Self-Righteousness

a. Seeing how God has reached out to humanity in ways everyone can understand and relate to
b. Relating and talking about God as Creator
c. Talking about God as Father
d. Building upon the promises of God

3. Avoiding the temptation to build walls
   a. The call to reach out
   b. Reaching out through common, everyday items and experiences
   c. Respecting differences while building connections

Week 6: Holy Living

1. Living the love of God
   a. Being of service
   b. Community and church service and evangelism
   c. Ways to reach out to other people
   d. Evangelizing without saying a word
   e. The importance of a life-witness

2. Holiness and evangelism
   a. Holiness for the believer, not the unbeliever
   b. Do not do what you hate...people are watching
   c. Using holiness as a tool for evangelism
   d. Living up to the Gospel in everyday life

TEXTBOOK ASSIGNMENTS

- Share an experience (4-6 sentences) about an experience you have had when someone was trying to evangelize to you – and it went awry. What happened? What did they do that was ineffective in reaching you?

- Share an experience (4-6 sentences) about an experience you had evangelizing someone else – and it went awry. Share what you have learned, now in hindsight, about that experience and what you could have done differently.

- Reach out to someone you know now (can be a stranger, can be a friend, etc.) and talk to them about the Lord – and tell us about your experience.

- Prepare an example of your testimony (either verbal or written) with us.

- In the back of the book, there are two sets of classes: One for New Disciples and one for Evangelism. Design your own New Disciples series of classes and your own Evangelism class for us, providing Bible verses, readings, and assignments you would give to those who would participate in it.

References

Introduction

[1]"Augustine Of Hippo>Quotes>Quotable Quotes."
https://www.goodreads.com/quotes/42572-because-god-has-made-us-
for-himself-our-hearts-are. Accessed on August 23, 2014.

Chapter 1

[1]"Mahatma Gandhi>Quotes>Quotable Quotes."
https://www.goodreads.com/quotes/22155-i-like-your-christ-i-do-not-like-
your-christians. Accessed on August 23, 2014.
[2]Strong's Exhaustive Concordance of the Bible, #3947
[3]Ibid., #5315

Chapter 2

[1]"The Humanity Of God Quotes."
https://www.goodreads.com/work/quotes/53171-the-humanity-of-god.
Accessed on August 23, 2014.

Chapter 3

[1]"Francis August Schaeffer>Quotes>Quotable Quote."
https://www.goodreads.com/quotes/239283-the-basic-problem-of-the-
christians-in-this-country-in. Accessed on August 23, 2014.

Chapter 5

[1]"David McGee>Quotes>Quotable Quote."

https://www.goodreads.com/quotes/454833-we-should-be-more-concerned-with-reaching-the-lost-than. Accessed on August 23, 2014.

Chapter 6

[1]"A Case For Joy." http://www.oneplace.com/ministries/a-new-beginning/read/articles/a-case-for-joy-9390.html. Accessed on August 23, 2014.

Chapter 7

[1]"Soren Kierkegaard>Quotes>Quotable Quote."
https://www.goodreads.com/quotes/160312-the-matter-is-quite-simple-the-bible-is-very-easy. Accessed on August 23, 2014.
[2]"Translation by Lambdin, Thomas O., from the Coptic Fragment. "Gospel of Thomas, The." http://www.sacred-texts.com/chr/thomas.htm. Available in the Public Domain. Accessed on August 21, 2014.

Chapter 8

[1]"Vikram Seth>Quotes>Quotable Quote."
https://www.goodreads.com/quotes/150628-god-save-us-from-people-who-mean-well. Accessed on August 23, 2014.

Chapter 10

[1]"Progidal Quotes."
http://www.brainyquote.com/quotes/keywords/prodigal.html. Accessed on August 24, 2014.
[2] From "Stepping Stones To Recovery," as found at http://www.therecoverygroup.org/jtr/letting_go.html. Accessed on August 24, 2014.

Chapter 11

[1]"Immanuel Kant>Quotes>Quotable Quotes."
https://www.goodreads.com/quotes/34329-seek-not-the-favor-of-the-multitude-it-is-seldom. Accessed on August 24, 2014.

Chapter 12

[1]"Evangelism Quotes."
http://www.tentmaker.org/Quotes/evangelismquotes.htm. Accessed on August 22, 2014.

Chapter 13

[1]"Evangelism Quotes."

http://www.tentmaker.org/Quotes/evangelismquotes.htm. Accessed on
August 22, 2014.

Chapter 14

[1]"Margaret Cho>Quotes>Quotable Quote."
https://www.goodreads.com/quotes/120598-i-want-jesus-to-come-back-
and-say-thats-not. Accessed on August 24, 2014.

Chapter 15

[1]"Evangelism Quotes."
http://www.tentmaker.org/Quotes/evangelismquotes.htm. Accessed on
August 22, 2014.

Chapter 16

[1]"Evangelism Quotes."
http://www.tentmaker.org/Quotes/evangelismquotes.htm. Accessed on
August 22, 2014.

About The Author

Dr. Lee Ann B. Marino, Ph.D., D.Min., D.D.

Apostle Dr. Lee Ann B. Marino, Ph.D., D.Min., D.D. (she/her) is "everyone's favorite theologian" leading Gen X, Millennials, and Gen Z with expertise in leadership training, queer and feminist theology, general religion, and apostolic theology. A graduate of Apostolic Preachers College, Dr. Marino has served in ministry since 1998 and was ordained as a pastor in 2002 and an apostle in 2010. She founded what is now Spitfire Apostolic Ministries in 2004. Under her ministry heading Dr. Marino is founder and overseer of Sanctuary International Fellowship Tabernacle – SIFT (the original home of National Coming Out Sunday) and Chancellor of Apostolic University.

Affectionately nicknamed "the Spitfire," Dr. Marino has spent over two decades as an "apostle, preacher, and teacher" (2 Timothy 1:11), exercising her personal mandate to become "all things to all people" (1 Corinthians 9:22). Her embrace of spiritual issues (both technical and intimate) has found its home among both seekers and believers, those who desire spiritual answers to today's issues.

Dr. Marino has preached throughout the United States, Puerto Rico, and Europe in hundreds of religious services and experiences throughout the years. A history maker in her own right, she has spent over two decades in advocacy, education, and work for and within minority spiritual communities (including African American, Hispanic, and LGBTQ+). She has also served as the first woman on all-male synods, councils, and panels, as well as the first preacher or speaker welcomed of a different race, sexual orientation, or identity among diverse communities. Today, Dr. Marino's work extends to over one hundred countries as she hosts the popular *Kingdom Now* podcast, which is in the top twenty percentile of all podcasts worldwide. She is also the author of over thirty books and the popular Patheos column, *Leadership on Fire*. To date, she has had four bestselling titles within their subject matter: *Understanding Demonology, Spiritual Warfare, Healing, and Deliverance: A Manual for the Christian Minister*; *Ministry School Boot Camp: Training for Helps Ministries, Appointments, and Beyond*; *Surrounded By So Great a Cloud of Witnesses: Women of Faith Who Revolutionized History*; and *Ministering to LGBTQs – and Those Who Love Them*.

As a public icon and social media influencer, Dr. Marino advocates for healthy body image (curvy/full-figured), queer representation (as a demisexual/aromantic), and albinism awareness, as a model. Known to those she works with, she is spiritual mom, teacher, leader, professor, confidant, and friend. She continues to transform, receiving new teaching, revelation, and insight in this thing we call "ministry." Through years of spiritual growth and maturity, Dr. Marino stands as herself, here to present what God has given to her for any who have an ear to hear.

For more information, visit her website at kingdompowernow.org.

www.ingramcontent.com/pod-product-compliance
Lightning Source LLC
Chambersburg PA
CBHW030008290326
41934CB00005B/265